D0031717

INAUGURAL ADDRESSES
OF THE PRESIDENTS
OF THE UNITED STATES
FROM W. H. TAFT
TO G.W. BUSH

The West Front of the U.S. Capitol at Clinton's inauguration,
January 20, 1993.

The Lakeside Classics

INAUGURAL ADDRESSES OF THE PRESIDENTS OF THE UNITED STATES FROM W. H. TAFT TO G.W. BUSH

EDITED BY

HENRY F. GRAFF

The Lakeside Press

R.R. DONNELLEY & SONS COMPANY
DECEMBER 2005

PUBLISHER'S PREFACE

In 1903, Thomas Elliott Donnelley, son of the company's founder, created the Lakeside Classics series because he believed that a simple book, distinctive and well-designed, was an appropriate holiday gift for our customers, employees, and friends. The first selection, *The Autobiography of Benjamin Franklin*, was an obvious choice for a U.S. printing company. But what next?

As T.E. Donnelley later wrote, "After the first volume, it was suggested by the editor that the inaugural addresses of the presidents should be brought together for a first time and published in the next two volumes." Thus, the company issued *Inaugural Addresses of the Presidents of the United States from Washington to Lincoln* (1904) and *from A. Johnson to T. Roosevelt* (1905). For collectors, these are two of the most difficult volumes in the series to find and two of the most expensive.

This year, exactly 100 years after the publication of the latter volume, we bring the sequence up to date with the inaugural addresses of presidents William Howard Taft through George Walker Bush. Returning to this theme has given us a unique opportunity to cover the events of the last century—achievements, from the building of the Panama Canal to the conquering of polio; explorations, from the first transatlantic flight to the moon landing; social change, from the campaign for rights by women to that by African Americans; and conflicts, from World War I through September 11, 2001, and the war in Iraq.

Advances in photography, digitization, and printing since 1905 have enabled us to produce a richly illustrated book containing some of the most memorable images of the past 100 years, in black and white and color. The digitized resources of the National Archives, including the Presidential Libraries, and the Library of Congress's National Digital Library provided many of these images. These remarkable national collections now are accessible through the Internet, a resource undreamed of in T.E. Donnelley's lifetime. We are also appreciative of The Avalon Project at Yale University, which graciously allowed us to download the digitized text of the addresses.

We thank our historical editor, Henry Franklin Graff, Ph.D., professor emeritus, department of history, Columbia University, for the introductory essay on the presidential inaugural address as a genre, the short biography of each president, and the essays preceding each inaugural address. Graff's specialties are U.S. diplomatic history and presidential history. His pioneering and popular seminar on the presidency was attended by presidents Truman and Ford. Among the books Graff has written are *The Presi-*

dents: *A Reference History* and *The Tuesday Cabinet: Deliberation and Decision on Peace and War under Lyndon B. Johnson.* President Johnson appointed Graff to the National Historical Publications Commission, reappointing him before leaving office. President Clinton appointed Graff to the John F. Kennedy Assassination Records Review Board.

We also thank Jacques Barzun, Ph.D., professor emeritus, history, Columbia University, for his comprehensive and critical reading of the Historical Introduction and the presidential essays.

This volume's presidential inaugural addresses portray a rapidly developing United States, expanding its reach beyond its borders to influence and be influenced by world events.

This past year RR Donnelley mirrored that kind of transformation, as we aggressively expanded our resources in the United States and dramatically increased our capabilities as a global provider. Every day, across multiple time zones, in various languages, following countless local business customs, RR Donnelley employees work to serve customers with products and services of exceptional quality.

In North America, we increased our ability to help customers prepare, produce, and deliver communications by investing to expand the flexibility and responsiveness of our diverse production facilities. Our plants installed new equipment, incorporated new systems to improve workflow efficiency, integrated digital production devices, and enhanced finishing capabilities. We acquired a printing facility in Charlestown, Indiana, that specializes in offset-printed tabloid-sized retail inserts, complementing our powerful gravure manufacturing capabilities, and enabling us to serve even better retailers' short- and long-run regional and national needs. We also built from the ground up a commercial printing facility in Atlanta, Georgia, that features state-of-the-art computer-driven equipment throughout.

In the Chicago area, we opened the world's largest private mail-handling facility, a 661,000-square-foot operation featuring sophisticated logistics capabilities and co-mailing lines that help our customers achieve the best postal rates. RR Donnelley now delivers into the United States Postal Service more than forty percent of all standard mail. Our Premedia Technologies business introduced new software systems and outsourcing services that help customers streamline processes used to prepare information to be printed and posted to Web sites. In expanding the number of our photography bays, we have become one of the largest providers of digital photography services in the United States.

Throughout the year, long-time customers renewed their relationships with RR Donnelley, and new customers chose us to help them achieve their purchasing, financial, regulatory compliance, communications, marketing, and other objectives. Many of these customers, global themselves, were attracted by our worldwide capabilities.

We invested in our existing facilities outside North America and also made important acquisitions. For example, acquiring Astron, a U.K.-based provider of document-based business process outsourcing services, nearly doubled our size in this fast-growing segment. Astron expands our capabilities for helping customers process, for example, responses to credit card solicitation mailings. Similarly, our acquisition of Asia Printers Group, Ltd. expanded our platform for producing books for export to worldwide markets and increased our ability to serve our Global Capital Markets customers in the Pacific Rim. We also acquired Poligrafia, one of Poland's largest printers of magazines, catalogs, retail inserts, and books, strengthening our ability to serve customers across Europe.

RR Donnelley is uniquely positioned to serve customers with the broadest range of products and services, across the broadest geographic range. The Internet and other communications technologies enable new ways of reducing customers' production cycle times. In 2005, we enhanced our digital printing networks, soft proofing capabilities for reviewing pages on a computer screen, and Internet-based print management and other tools, all of which work in concert to make RR Donnelley as agile in serving customers from our global network as if each of our facilities was practically next door. We can transcend physical proximity to provide our customers with crucial speed-to-market advantages.

Since early 2004, when RR Donnelley completed the acquisition of Moore Wallace, the company has been transformed: adding thousands of employees via acquisition, taking on new product lines, and integrating established brands into its own. Guiding this fast growth are the core values that have always characterized RR Donnelley: integrity and genuine care for our customers, employees, communities, shareholders, and other stakeholders.

These values were apparent in 2005 as we continued to achieve important safety milestones. Our people—our most precious asset—worked together to develop processes and comply with procedures that minimize the risk of injury. RR Donnelley facilities across the world set marks for exceptional safety performance. Among all the financial and other measurements we track, none are more important than those that indicate that we are providing a safe workplace.

We also follow processes to assure that we deliver great quality in products and services. We were especially pleased that judges evaluating entries for prestigious printing awards recognized the caliber of our work. For example, this year RR Donnelley received 55 Gold Ink Awards—more than twice as many as any other printer—for exceptional quality of magazines, annual reports, books, and more.

We work to be good neighbors, not only in the communities in which we live and work, but also to our environment. We do this by ensuring we have the programs, practices, and resources to help us protect our people and to preserve our environment. As evidence, one more facility became certified to the internationally recognized ISO 14001 specification for environmental management, and another was certified to OSHA's Voluntary Protection Program. In addition, we continue to embrace programs that allow us to certify that the materials we use for our customers meet certain environmental standards.

RR Donnelley combines a rich tradition of quality and craftsmanship with a forward-looking approach that embraces innovation. Although we provide our customers with very different kinds of products and serve them across much broader geographies than when we last published a collection of inaugural addresses, we address them with the same care, attention, and integrity that always have distinguished RR Donnelley.

Last spring, our corporate headquarters moved to more economical space in a new building in downtown Chicago. Customers and other visitors to our headquarters enjoy seeing our historic collection of books, magazines, catalogs, directories, and other materials dating to the 1860s. The collection vividly portrays RR Donnelley's respect for our heritage and commitment to quality. This, our sixth home, is within ten blocks of the building where T.E. Donnelley printed the first Lakeside Classics in 1903.

———

We note with appreciation the RR Donnelley Board members who retired this year: Gregory Q. Brown, James R. Donnelley, Alfred C. Eckert III, and Joan D. Manley. Jim Donnelley, great-grandson of our founder, merits special recognition and thanks for his lifetime of service to the company. Jim joined RR Donnelley in 1962 in sales and retired from active employment in 2000 as Vice Chairman. In recognition of his 29 years of service on the board, he was named Director Emeritus.

As we stand on the threshold of a new year, we wish you and your loved ones peace, good health and happiness.

THE PUBLISHER
December 2005

Contents

Contents

Contents

Contents

Illustrations

Illustrations

Illustrations

Illustrations

Historical Introduction

Presidential inaugurations are the moments when the nation resets its goals and reconfirms its ideals. A new president's face becomes the face of the country and his actions the subject of public and private discussion and foreign speculation. Few other nations have a comparably picturesque ceremony for the transfer of power. On inauguration day the president—celebrated by military units marching in tribute to him and cheered by a huge crowd of political supporters when he comes down the Capitol steps to the place of honor on the platform—is the chief of state, not the chief of government.

When Washington gave the first inaugural address, he spoke indoors to members of Congress, thus conducting himself similarly to a British king opening a session of Parliament. Since then each new president has been seen at his inauguration as an already historic figure, rather like a monarch at his coronation. But, unlike the crowning of a king, investing the president-elect into office takes only five minutes. On inauguration day, the incoming president embodies the immortal sentiment Jefferson offered in his inaugural: "We are all Republicans, we are all Federalists." He is fleetingly the American people incarnate. But on the morrow, he is again a political partisan.

Inaugurations have taken place every fourth year since 1789, when the constitutional republic came into being. It is the periodic beat of time in U.S. politics. The possibility that a new election should be held after a president dies in office, thus breaking the regularity, was killed in 1841. When President William Henry Harrison perished just a month after his inauguration, Vice President John Tyler, calling himself president, moved into the White House. Ex-president John Quincy Adams, close student of government that he was, regarded Tyler as "Vice President acting as President" and questioned whether he "has the right to occupy the president's house or draw his salary." No framer of the Constitution was still alive to say what the delegates in Philadelphia had had in mind for such a situation, supposing they had considered it at all. Tyler's claiming the office was never heavily challenged, so the only threat to the four-year rhythm was over.

March 4 was established as the date for inauguration by an act adopted by the Continental Congress on September 13, 1788. Responsive to the slowness and difficulty of travel, it provided that the first Wednesday in the following March—which proved to be the fourth—should be the day for inaugurating the new national government under the Constitution. Since even by March 4, 1789, too few members of Congress had arrived in New York to form a quorum and begin proceedings, George

Washington's Inauguration, 1789; oil painting by Allyn Cox. Mural depicts (from center left) Robert R. Livingston, chancellor of New York State; Senate Secretary Samuel Otis (holding Bible); Washington; and Vice President John Adams.

Washington was not inaugurated until April 30.

From his time on, every inauguration took place in March until Franklin Roosevelt's second swearing-in in 1937. By that year, the Twentieth Amendment to the Constitution was in force. Adopted October 15, 1933, it recognized that such a long stretch of time between election day and the actual commencement of work was no longer necessary. The new date it fixed was January 20. As the Senate Committee on the Judiciary explained: "Under present conditions [of communication and transportation] the result of elections is known all over the country within a few hours after the polls close, and the Capital City is within a few days' travel of the remotest portions of the country . . . . "

Another problem with the inaugural calendar— when the mandated inauguration day falls on a Sunday—has been solved by custom, not legislation. It first happened to James Monroe, on Sunday, March 4, 1821. Since it was considered inappropriate to hold a festive celebration on the Christian Sabbath, a private oath-taking was held on the required date and the public ceremony not until the next day. This tradition continues to the present. An unusual variant on this practice took place following the disputed election of 1876, in which the majority of the Electoral College went to Republican Rutherford B. Hayes although Democrat Samuel Tilden had the most popular votes.

Plans were made for the public swearing-in of Hayes to take place on Monday, March 5, 1877. But General Grant, the outgoing president, earnestly believed that it could be disastrous for the country to be without a president for one day. So he invited the president-elect and his family to a gala dinner at the White House on Saturday, March 3. Before the meal began, Hayes was ushered into the Red Room and secretly sworn in by the chief justice. None of the guests knew in advance what was afoot.

The inaugural address, usually delivered immediately after the president-elect has taken the oath of office, is the high point of every inauguration. It should be noted, though, that several presidents—John Adams, Thomas Jefferson, James Polk, Zachary Taylor, Abraham Lincoln, James Garfield, and Grover Cleveland—were sworn in *after* their addresses—as if to confirm their resolve on the words they had just spoken to the nation. Almost always the oath is taken while standing before the chief justice of the United States, with the right hand of the president-elect laid on a Bible. Generally, the chief justice offers the oath phrase by phrase, to be repeated by the president-elect, but occasionally—as, for instance, Franklin Roosevelt did in 1933—the words are spoken consecutively by the new chief executive. The new president then adds "So help me God," picks up the holy volume, and kisses it. (John Quincy Adams, who once compared with Holy Scriptures the diary he kept for a lifetime, took the oath in 1825 on a volume of the laws of the United States.) The dramatic appeal to the Divine is not found in the Constitution but was uttered by Washington and, in conformity with him, by all his successors, who sometimes also use the very same Bible he held. The oath, which begins: "I do solemnly swear (or affirm) . . . " allows a president to *affirm* the pledge if he holds a religious belief that forbids swearing. For reasons not clear, Franklin Pierce in 1853 affirmed the words of the oath.

An inauguration offers few of the colorful details that sparkle at royal coronations. Still, as soon as the president enters the scene, the Marine Band, known since its establishment by President John Adams on July 11, 1798, as the "President's Own," plays four "Ruffles and Flourishes"—the ruffles on drums and the flourishes on bugles—and then "Hail to the Chief." This song did not begin as a presidential tune. Possibly adapted from an old Scottish air, it is credited to an English songsmith named James Sanderson, who wrote it for a stage presentation of Sir Walter Scott's *The Lady of the Lake*. The first time it was played to honor a president was in 1815 to mark Washington's birthday—sixteen years after his death. It honored a living president for the first time when John Quincy Adams was invited on July 4, 1828, to turn the first shovelful of soil for the construction of the Chesapeake and Ohio Canal. The

Stereographic image of Rutherford B. Hayes's public inauguration ceremony, Monday, March 5, 1877.

first inauguration it adorned was Martin Van Buren's in 1837. Two First Ladies gave it familiarity: Mrs. John (Letitia Christian) Tyler, who wished her husband to be greeted by the song whenever he appeared as commander in chief, and Mrs. James K. (Sarah Childress) Polk, who was eager to see her husband noticed, had it played frequently when he appeared in public.

In Lincoln's day, the playing of "Hail to the Chief" was almost always followed by "Hail Columbia." This song, the first U.S. national anthem, was composed by Philip Hile, a German-American violinist, for Washington's inauguration in 1789. Called the "President's March," it was renamed "Hail Columbia" by Joseph Hopkinson, who wrote the words in 1798. In 2005 its playing opened the inauguration ceremony of Vice President Richard B. Cheney.

President Chester A. Arthur, who replaced James A. Garfield upon his death in 1881, regarded "Hail to the Chief" as inelegant and therefore undignified; he instructed John Philip Sousa, the Marine Band leader, to write a more satisfactory tune. Sousa produced an arresting piece called "Presidential Polonaise," but it had no allure. When Grover Cleveland came to the White House in 1885, he almost immediately reestablished "Hail to the Chief" as the appropriate presidential fanfare. In 1954, the Department of Defense made "Hail to the Chief" the official musical tribute at presidential events. The public does not know the words of the song yet responds warmly to its playing.

The installation of the vice president is less dramatic. The brief inauguration speeches delivered by new vice presidents are barely recorded and are historically inconsequential. The explanation, John Adams declared, was that the vice presidency, which he held under Washington, is invested with "two separate powers—the one *in esse* and the other *in posse*." (*In esse*, that is, in being, it is nothing; but *in posse*, in potential, it is everything.) Most unusual has been the public swearing-in of recent vice presidents. Historically, vice presidents-elect were inaugurated indoors in the Capitol and arrived at the presidential swearing-in already sworn in themselves. This reflected the fact that most presidents and their vice presidents were not intimates. Usually the vice president was placed on the party ticket simply to balance it geographically or politically.

A few presidents acknowledged their vice presidents in public. James Monroe in 1817 and 1821 rode to his inauguration with Vice President Daniel Tompkins, and Harry Truman rode with Alben Barkley in the inauguration parade in 1949. It is worth noting, however, that after the early vice presidents, including George Clinton of New York, who was elected under Thomas Jefferson and James Madison, and John C. Calhoun, who also was elected twice—first under John Quincy Adams and then under Andrew Jackson—no vice president was reelected until Thomas Marshall of Indiana, who served in Wilson's two terms, from 1913–21.

Regarding the inauguration and inaugural address, the public is so much aware of the tradition surrounding the event that any change, large or small, is observed and reported upon in the press. There are many examples: In 1809, for the first time, an inaugural ball was held in Washington to honor a president—James Madison. John Quincy Adams became the first president to wear long pants instead of knee britches to his inauguration. Monroe in 1817 held the first inauguration out-of-doors. Lady Bird Johnson held the Bible on which Lyndon Baines Johnson was sworn in in 1965—the first time that a First Lady had participated in the ceremony. Ronald Reagan, with his instinct for originality, moved the ceremony from the east to the west side of the Capitol in 1981—creating a practice followed since.

It is a moving tradition that the outgoing president attends the inauguration of his successor. On inauguration day the president-elect picks up the retiring president at the White House, and together they ride to the Capitol. The first such pair was Jackson and Van Buren in 1837, who, incidentally, traveled in a carriage crafted from the timbers of the heroic frigate *Constitution,* known affectionately as "Old Ironsides." On only three occasions has the

Umbrellas shield attendees from drenching rain during Benjamin Harrison's swearing-in ceremony on the East Side of the U.S. Capitol, March 4, 1889.

outgoing president been absent from his successor's inauguration: John Adams was not present at Jefferson's in 1801, nor did John Quincy Adams attend Jackson's in 1829. Andrew Johnson held his last cabinet meeting at the White House right up until noon, March 4, 1869, thus keeping himself and his inner circle from watching Grant become president. In contrast, at Harrison's oath-taking in 1889 in a drenching rain, Cleveland kindly held an umbrella over the incoming president who had defeated him.

Traveling from the White House to the Capitol and back for the great ceremony is also noteworthy: Jefferson in 1801 and Jackson in 1829 both walked to the Capitol from their homes. Harrison in 1841 rode a horse in both directions—and, wearing no coat on a freezing day, he may have hastened his fatal illness. William Howard Taft in 1909 was the first newly installed president to have his wife accompany him in his carriage when he left the Capitol after the inauguration. In 1921, Warren Gamaliel Harding and Woodrow Wilson rode to the Capitol in an automobile, ending the established habit of conveying the new president and his predecessor in a horse and carriage. Jimmy Carter after his inauguration in 1977 walked with his wife and daughter from the Capitol to the White House.

Inaugurations always have been media events. This attention does not corrupt them; it adorns them. That they are now seen by millions of people and recorded and pictured in history books testifies to their immense importance. The public's involvement, however, has changed greatly over the years. In 1801, on the day before his oath-taking, Jefferson made his inaugural address available to a Washington newspaper. Before his swearing-in was over, boys outside the Capitol were selling newspapers containing the full text. Forty years later, Harrison's ninety-minute inaugural was the first sent immediately to several parts of the country by railroad. That same evening, people in Philadelphia were able to read the speech. The first inauguration photographed was Buchanan's in 1857 (actually, it was a blurry daguerreotype), and the first to be shot by a motion-picture camera was William McKinley's forty years later. Calvin Coolidge's inaugural was the first heard on radio; Harry Truman's inauguration was the first seen on television.

The inaugural addresses in this volume, regardless of tenor or quality, are choice documents of American history. They are salutes to the people. All of them look to the future with hope and confidence and, only occasionally, with foreboding.

Henry F. Graff
Professor Emeritus of History
Columbia University
New York, New York
June 2005

INAUGURAL ADDRESSES
OF THE PRESIDENTS
OF THE UNITED STATES
FROM W. H. TAFT
TO G.W. BUSH

William Howard Taft

27th President of the United States
1909–13

William Howard Taft

BORN: September 15, 1857, Cincinnati, Ohio
MARRIED: Helen "Nellie" Herron, June 19, 1886;
three children
DIED: March 8, 1930, Washington, D.C.
PARTY: Republican
EDUCATION: Yale College (1878); Cincinnati Law
School (1880).

CAREER:
Various Republican judicial appointments; civil governor of the Philippines (1901–04); Theodore Roosevelt's secretary of war (1904–08); president (1909–13); professor of law at Yale University (1913–21); chief justice of the United States (1921–30).

PRESIDENTIAL CAMPAIGNS:
1908: Defeated Democrat William Jennings Bryant on Bryant's third presidential attempt.
1912: Lost to Democrat Woodrow Wilson in a three-party race in which Theodore Roosevelt deserted him for the Progressive ticket.

President Taft speaks at Manassas (Virginia) Court House, November 10, 1911.

INTRODUCTION

William Howard Taft had never stood for election before his 1908 presidential campaign. A zealous choice of Theodore Roosevelt to be his successor, Taft would have preferred appointment to the Supreme Court, but his wife was ardent to see him in the White House.

Not an accomplished politician, Taft turned his inaugural speech into a presentation of his agenda as chief executive, offering words that would have been worthier of the campaign. His attention to minute details—for example, his close examination of the kind of locks the Panama Canal required—must surely have seemed out of place on an occasion designed to start a new time in the country's life. Further, his insistent reference to his predecessor suggested not only his gratitude to his sponsor, but that he was filling in for Teddy and not yet his own man.

The excessively long speech must have bored his audience that was much smaller than usual at inaugurations because a storm dropped ten inches of snow on Washington. The terrible weather even caused the ceremony to be brought indoors. Taft said grimly: "I knew it would be a cold day when I got to be president." He realized his life's dream when President Harding appointed him chief justice of the United States in 1921.

William Howard Taft
Inaugural Address

Thursday, March 4, 1909

My Fellow Citizens:
Anyone who has taken the oath I have just taken must feel a heavy weight of responsibility. If not, he has no conception of the powers and duties of the office upon which he is about to enter, or he is lacking in a proper sense of the obligation which the oath imposes.

The office of an inaugural address is to give a summary outline of the main policies of the new administration, so far as they can be anticipated. I have had the honor to be one of the advisers of my distinguished predecessor,[1] and, as such, to hold up his hands in the reforms he has initiated. I should be untrue to myself, to my promises, and to the declarations of the party platform upon which I was elected to office, if I did not make the maintenance and enforcement of those reforms a most important feature of my administration. They were directed to the suppression of the lawlessness and abuses of power of the great combinations of capital invested in railroads and in industrial enterprises carrying on interstate commerce. The steps which my predeces-

---

1. Theodore Roosevelt, twenty-sixth president, 1901–09.

sor took and the legislation passed on his recommendation have accomplished much, have caused a general halt in the vicious policies which created popular alarm, and have brought about in the business affected a much higher regard for existing law.

To render the reforms lasting, however, and to secure at the same time freedom from alarm on the part of those pursuing proper and progressive business methods, further legislative and executive action are needed. Relief of the railroads from certain restrictions of the antitrust law have been urged by my predecessor and will be urged by me. On the other hand, the administration is pledged to legislation looking to a proper federal supervision and restriction to prevent excessive issues of bonds and stock by companies owning and operating interstate commerce railroads.

Then, too, a reorganization of the Department of Justice, of the Bureau of Corporations in the Department of Commerce and Labor, and of the Interstate Commerce Commission, looking to effective cooperation of these agencies, is needed to secure a more rapid and certain enforcement of the laws affecting interstate railroads and industrial combinations.

I hope to be able to submit at the first regular session of the incoming Congress, in December next, definite suggestions in respect to the needed amendments to the antitrust and the interstate commerce law and the changes required in the executive departments concerned in their enforcement.

It is believed that with the changes to be recommended American business can be assured of that measure of stability and certainty in respect to those things that may be done and those that are prohibited which is essential to the life and growth of all business. Such a plan must include the right of the people to avail themselves of those methods of combining capital and effort deemed necessary to reach the highest degree of economic efficiency, at the same time differentiating between combinations based upon legitimate economic reasons and those formed with the intent of creating monopolies and artificially controlling prices.

The work of formulating into practical shape such changes is creative work of the highest order, and requires all the deliberation possible in the interval. I believe that the amendments to be proposed are just as necessary in the protection of legitimate business as in the clinching of the reforms which properly bear the name of my predecessor.

A matter of most pressing importance is the revision of the tariff. In accordance with the promises of the platform upon which I was elected, I shall call Congress into extra session to meet on the fifteenth day of March, in order that consideration may be at once given to a bill revising the Dingley Act.[2] This

---

2. Passed in 1897, the Dingley Act set high tariffs on imported goods.

should secure an adequate revenue and adjust the duties in such a manner as to afford to labor and to all industries in this country, whether of the farm, mine or factory, protection by tariff equal to the difference between the cost of production abroad and the cost of production here, and have a provision which shall put into force, upon executive determination of certain facts, a higher or maximum tariff against those countries whose trade policy toward us equitably requires such discrimination. It is thought that there has been such a change in conditions since the enactment of the Dingley Act, drafted on a similarly protective principle, that the measure of the tariff above stated will permit the reduction of rates in certain schedules and will require the advancement of few, if any.

The proposal to revise the tariff made in such an authoritative way as to lead the business community to count upon it necessarily halts all those branches of business directly affected; and as these are most important, it disturbs the whole business of the country. It is imperatively necessary, therefore, that a tariff bill be drawn in good faith in accordance with promises made before the election by the party in power, and as promptly passed as due consideration will permit. It is not that the tariff is more important in the long run than the perfecting of the reforms in respect to antitrust legislation and interstate commerce regulation, but the need for action when the revision of the tariff has been determined upon is more immediate to avoid embarrassment of business. To secure the needed speed in the passage of the tariff bill, it would seem wise to attempt no other legislation at the extra session. I venture this as a suggestion only, for the course to be taken by Congress, upon the call of the Executive, is wholly within its discretion.

In the making of a tariff bill the prime motive is taxation and the securing thereby of a revenue. Due largely to the business depression which followed the financial panic of 1907, the revenue from customs and other sources has decreased to such an extent that the expenditures for the current fiscal year will exceed the receipts by $100,000,000. It is imperative that such a deficit shall not continue, and the framers of the tariff bill must, of course, have in mind the total revenues likely to be produced by it and so arrange the duties as to secure an adequate income. Should it be impossible to do so by import duties, new kinds of taxation must be adopted, and among these I recommend a graduated inheritance tax as correct in principle and as certain and easy of collection.

The obligation on the part of those responsible for the expenditures made to carry on the Government, to be as economical as possible, and to make the burden of taxation as light as possible, is plain, and should be affirmed in every declaration of government policy. This is especially true when we are face to face with a heavy deficit. But when the desire to win the popular approval leads to the cutting off of expenditures really needed to make the government effective and to enable it to accomplish its proper objects, the result is as much to be condemned as the waste of government funds in unnecessary expenditure. The scope of a modern government in what it can and ought to accomplish for its people has been widened far beyond the principles laid down by the old laissez-faire school of political writers, and this widening has met popular approval.

In the Department of Agriculture the use of scientific experiments on a large scale and the spread of information derived from them for the improvement of general agriculture must go on.

The importance of supervising business of great railways and industrial combinations and the necessary investigation and prosecution of unlawful business methods are another necessary tax upon government which did not exist half a century ago.

The putting into force of laws which shall secure the conservation of our resources, so far as they may be within the jurisdiction of the federal government, including the most important work of saving and restoring our forests and the great improvement of waterways, are all proper government functions which must involve large expenditure if properly performed. While some of them, like the reclamation of arid lands, are made to pay for themselves, others are of such an indirect benefit that this cannot be expected of them. A permanent improvement, like the Panama Canal,[3] should be treated as a distinct enterprise, and should be paid for by the proceeds of bonds, the issue of which will distribute its cost between the present and future generations in accordance with the benefits derived. It may well be submitted to the serious consideration of Congress whether the deepening and control of the channel of a great river system, like that of the Ohio or of the Mississippi, when definite and practical plans for the enterprise have been approved and determined upon, should not be provided for in the same way.

Then, too, there are expenditures of government absolutely necessary if our country is to maintain its proper place among the nations of the world, and is to exercise its proper influence in defense of its own trade interests in the maintenance of traditional American policy against the colonization of European monarchies in this hemi-

---

3. The canal connects the Atlantic and Pacific oceans by means of a series of locks across the Isthmus of Panama in Central America. Construction was begun by the French in 1881. The French assets were acquired by the United States in 1903. After ten years of construction on a monumental scale, the canal was informally opened to shipping traffic on August 15, 1914.

sphere, and in the promotion of peace and international morality. I refer to the cost of maintaining a proper army, a proper navy, and suitable fortifications upon the mainland of the United States and in its dependencies.

We should have an army so organized and so officered as to be capable in time of emergency, in cooperation with the national militia and under the provisions of a proper national volunteer law, rapidly to expand into a force sufficient to resist all probable invasion from abroad and to furnish a respectable expeditionary force if necessary in the maintenance of our traditional American policy which bears the name of President Monroe.[4]

Our fortifications are yet in a state of only partial completeness, and the number of men to man them is insufficient. In a few years however, the usual annual appropriations for our coast defenses, both on the mainland and in the dependencies, will make them sufficient to resist all direct attack, and by that time we may hope that the men to man them will be provided as a necessary adjunct. The distance of our shores from Europe and Asia of course reduces the necessity for maintaining under

4. The Monroe Doctrine: In 1823, President James Monroe warned European powers that "the American continents, by the free and independent condition which they have assumed and maintain, are henceforth not to be considered as subjects for future colonization by any European power."

arms a great army, but it does not take away the requirement of mere prudence—that we should have an army sufficiently large and so constituted as to form a nucleus out of which a suitable force can quickly grow.

What has been said of the army may be affirmed in even a more emphatic way of the navy. A modern navy can not be improvised. It must be built and in existence when the emergency arises which calls for its use and operation. My distinguished predecessor has in many speeches and messages set out with great force and striking language the necessity for maintaining a strong navy commensurate with the coast line, the governmental resources, and the foreign trade of our nation; and I wish to reiterate all the reasons which he has presented in favor of the policy of maintaining a strong navy as the best conservator of our peace with other nations, and the best means of securing respect for the assertion of our rights, the defense of our interests, and the exercise of our influence in international matters.

Our international policy is always to promote peace. We shall enter into any war with a full consciousness of the awful consequences that it always entails, whether successful or not, and we, of course, shall make every effort consistent with national honor and the highest national interest to avoid a resort to arms. We favor every instrumentality, like that of the Hague Tribunal[5] and arbitration treaties made with a view to its use in all international controversies, in order to maintain peace and to avoid war. But we should be blind to existing conditions and should allow ourselves to become foolish idealists if we did not realize that, with all the nations of the world armed and prepared for war, we must be ourselves in a similar condition, in order to prevent other nations from taking advantage of us and of our inability to defend our interests and assert our rights with a strong hand.

In the international controversies that are likely to arise in the Orient growing out of the question of the open door and other issues[6] the United States can maintain her interests intact and can secure respect for her just demands. She will not be able to do so, however, if it is understood that she never intends to back up her assertion of right and her defense of her interest by anything but mere verbal protest and diplomatic note. For these reasons the expenses of the army and navy and of coast defenses should always be considered as something which the government must pay for, and they should not be cut off through mere consideration of economy.

5. The Permanent Court of Arbitration was established in The Hague, the Netherlands, in 1899.
6. The United States advocated an Open Door Policy (1899), by which all nations would have equal trading and development rights in China.

Our government is able to afford a suitable army and a suitable navy. It may maintain them without the slightest danger to the republic or the cause of free institutions, and fear of additional taxation ought not to change a proper policy in this regard.

The policy of the United States in the Spanish war[7] and since has given it a position of influence among the nations that it never had before, and should be constantly exerted to securing to its bona fide citizens, whether native or naturalized, respect for them as such in foreign countries. We should make every effort to prevent humiliating and degrading prohibition against any of our citizens wishing temporarily to sojourn in foreign countries because of race or religion.

The admission of Asiatic immigrants who cannot be amalgamated with our population has been made the subject either of prohibitory clauses in our treaties and statutes or of strict administrative regulation secured by diplomatic negotiation. I sincerely hope that we may continue to minimize the evils likely to arise from such immigration without unnecessary friction and by mutual concessions between self-respecting governments. Meantime we must take every precaution to prevent, or failing that, to punish outbursts of race feeling among our people against foreigners of whatever nationality

---

7. Spanish-American War, 1898.

Taft, accompanied by President Theodore Roosevelt, drives through a snowstorm to his inauguration, March 4, 1909.

who have by our grant a treaty right to pursue lawful business here and to be protected against lawless assault or injury.

This leads me to point out a serious defect in the present federal jurisdiction, which ought to be remedied at once. Having assured to other countries by treaty the protection of our laws for such of their subjects or citizens as we permit to come within our jurisdiction, we now leave to a state or a city, not under the control of the federal government, the duty of performing our international obligations in this respect. By proper legislation we may, and ought to, place in the hands of the federal Executive the means of enforcing the treaty rights of such aliens in the courts of the federal government. It puts our government in a pusillanimous position to make definite engagements to protect aliens and then to excuse the failure to perform those engagements by an explanation that the duty to keep them is in states or cities, not within our control. If we would promise we must put ourselves in a position to perform our promise. We cannot permit the possible failure of justice, due to local prejudice in any state or municipal government, to expose us to the risk of a war which might be avoided if federal jurisdiction was asserted by suitable legislation by Congress and carried out by proper proceedings instituted by the Executive in the courts of the national government.

One of the reforms to be carried out during the incoming administration is a change of our monetary and banking laws, so as to secure greater elasticity in the forms of currency available for trade and to prevent the limitations of law from operating to increase the embarrassment of a financial panic. The monetary commission, lately appointed, is giving full consideration to existing conditions and to all proposed remedies, and will doubtless suggest one that will meet the requirements of business and of public interest.

We may hope that the report will embody neither the narrow view of those who believe that the sole purpose of the new system should be to secure a large return on banking capital or of those who would have greater expansion of currency with little regard to provisions for its immediate redemption or ultimate security. There is no subject of economic discussion so intricate and so likely to evoke differing views and dogmatic statements as this one. The commission, in studying the general influence of currency on business and of business on currency, have wisely extended their investigations in European banking and monetary methods. The information that they have derived from such experts as they have found abroad will undoubtedly be found helpful in the solution of the difficult problem they have in hand.

The incoming Congress should promptly fulfill

the promise of the Republican platform and pass a proper postal savings bank bill. It will not be unwise or excessive paternalism. The promise to repay by the government will furnish an inducement to savings deposits which private enterprise can not supply and at such a low rate of interest as not to withdraw custom from existing banks. It will substantially increase the funds available for investment as capital in useful enterprises. It will furnish absolute security which makes the proposed scheme of government guaranty of deposits so alluring, without its pernicious results.

I sincerely hope that the incoming Congress will be alive, as it should be, to the importance of our foreign trade and of encouraging it in every way feasible. The possibility of increasing this trade in the Orient, in the Philippines, and in South America are known to everyone who has given the matter attention. The direct effect of free trade between this country and the Philippines will be marked upon our sales of cottons, agricultural machinery, and other manufactures. The necessity of the establishment of direct lines of steamers between North and South America has been brought to the attention of Congress by my predecessor and by Mr. Root[8] before and after his noteworthy visit to that

8. Elihu Root (1845–1937) served under President McKinley as secretary of war and under President Theodore Roosevelt as secretary of war, then secretary of state. He was appointed to the U.S. Senate from New York in 1909. Root received the Nobel Peace Prize in 1912.

continent, and I sincerely hope that Congress may be induced to see the wisdom of a tentative effort to establish such lines by the use of mail subsidies.

The importance of the part which the Departments of Agriculture and of Commerce and Labor may play in ridding the markets of Europe of prohibitions and discriminations against the importation of our products is fully understood, and it is hoped that the use of the maximum and minimum feature of our tariff law to be soon passed will be effective to remove many of those restrictions.

The Panama Canal will have a most important bearing upon the trade between the eastern and far western sections of our country, and will greatly increase the facilities for transportation between the eastern and the western seaboard, and may possibly revolutionize the transcontinental rates with respect to bulky merchandise. It will also have a most beneficial effect to increase the trade between the eastern seaboard of the United States and the western coast of South America, and, indeed, with some of the important ports on the east coast of South America reached by rail from the west coast.

The work on the canal is making most satisfactory progress. The type of the canal as a lock canal was fixed by Congress after a full consideration of the conflicting reports of the majority and minority of the consulting board, and after the recommendation of the War Department and the Executive

Construction of the Gatun Locks on the Panama Canal.

upon those reports. Recent suggestion that something had occurred on the Isthmus to make the lock type of the canal less feasible than it was supposed to be when the reports were made and the policy determined on led to a visit to the Isthmus of a board of competent engineers to examine the Gatun dam and locks, which are the key of the lock type.

The report of that board shows nothing has occurred in the nature of newly revealed evidence which should change the views once formed in the original discussion. The construction will go on under a most effective organization controlled by Colonel Goethals[9] and his fellow army engineers associated with him, and will certainly be completed early in the next administration, if not before.

Some type of canal must be constructed. The lock type has been selected. We are all in favor of having it built as promptly as possible. We must not now, therefore, keep up a fire in the rear of the agents whom we have authorized to do our work on the Isthmus. We must hold up their hands, and speaking for the incoming administration I wish to say that I propose to devote all the energy possible and under my control to pushing of this work on the plans which have been adopted, and to stand

9. George Washington Goethals (1858–1928) was chairman and chief engineer of the Isthmian Canal Commission, overseeing the construction of the Panama Canal. On its completion, he became governor of the Panama Canal Zone until 1916.

behind the men who are doing faithful, hard work to bring about the early completion of this, the greatest constructive enterprise of modern times.

The governments of our dependencies in Puerto Rico and the Philippines are progressing as favorably as could be desired. The prosperity of Puerto Rico continues unabated. The business conditions in the Philippines are not all that we could wish them to be, but with the passage of the new tariff bill permitting free trade between the United States and the archipelago, with such limitations on sugar and tobacco as shall prevent injury to domestic interests in those products, we can count on an improvement in business conditions in the Philippines and the development of a mutually profitable trade between this country and the islands. Meantime our government in each dependency is upholding the traditions of civil liberty and increasing popular control which might be expected under American auspices. The work which we are doing there redounds to our credit as a nation.

I look forward with hope to increasing the already good feeling between the South and the other sections of the country. My chief purpose is not to effect a change in the electoral vote of the southern states. That is a secondary consideration. What I look forward to is an increase in the tolerance of political views of all kinds and their advocacy throughout the South, and the existence of a respectable political opposition in every state; even more than this, to an increased feeling on the part of all the people in the South that this government is their government, and that its officers in their states are their officers.

The consideration of this question can not, however, be complete and full without reference to the Negro race, its progress and its present condition. The Thirteenth Amendment secured them freedom; the Fourteenth Amendment due process of law, protection of property, and the pursuit of happiness; and the Fifteenth Amendment attempted to secure the Negro against any deprivation of the privilege to vote because he was a Negro. The Thirteenth and Fourteenth Amendments have been generally enforced and have secured the objects for which they are intended. While the Fifteenth Amendment has not been generally observed in the past, it ought to be observed, and the tendency of southern legislation today is toward the enactment of electoral qualifications which shall square with that amendment. Of course, the mere adoption of a constitutional law is only one step in the right direction. It must be fairly and justly enforced as well. In time both will come. Hence it is clear to all that the domination of an ignorant, irresponsible element can be prevented by constitutional laws which shall exclude from voting both Negroes and whites not having education or other qualifications thought to be necessary for a proper electorate. The danger of the control of an ignorant electorate has therefore passed. With this change, the interest which many of the southern white citizens take in the welfare of the Negroes has increased. The colored men must base their hope on the results of their own industry, self-restraint, thrift, and business success, as well as upon the aid and comfort and sympathy which they may receive from their white neighbors of the South.

There was a time when northerners who sympathized with the Negro in his necessary struggle for better conditions sought to give him the suffrage as a protection to enforce its exercise against the prevailing sentiment of the South. The movement proved to be a failure. What remains is the Fifteenth Amendment to the Constitution and the right to have statutes of states specifying qualifications for electors subjected to the test of compliance with that amendment. This is a great protection to the Negro. It never will be repealed, and it never ought to be repealed. If it had not passed, it might be difficult now to adopt it; but with it in our fundamental law, the policy of southern legislation must and will tend to obey it, and so long as the statutes of the states meet the test of this amendment and are not otherwise in conflict with the Constitution and laws of the United States, it is not the disposition or within the province of the federal government to interfere with the regulation by southern states of their domestic affairs. There is in the South a stronger feeling than ever among the intelligent well to do and influential element in favor of the industrial education of the Negro and the encouragement of the race to make themselves useful members of the community. The progress which the Negro has made in the last fifty years, from slavery, when its statistics are reviewed, is marvelous, and it furnishes every reason to hope that in the next twenty-five years a still greater improvement in his condition as a productive member of society, on the farm, and in the shop, and in other occupations may come.

The Negroes are now Americans. Their ancestors came here years ago against their will, and this is their only country and their only flag. They have shown themselves anxious to live for it and to die for it. Encountering the race feeling against them, subjected at times to cruel injustice growing out of it, they may well have our profound sympathy and aid in the struggle they are making. We are charged with the sacred duty of making their path as smooth and easy as we can. Any recognition of their distinguished men, any appointment to office from among their number, is properly taken as an encouragement and an appreciation of their progress, and this just policy should be pursued when suitable occasion offers.

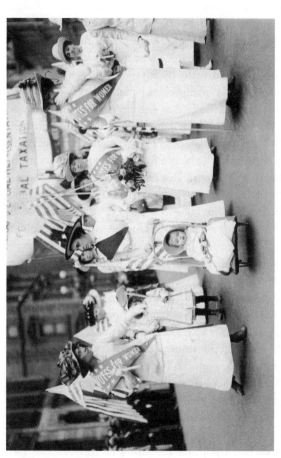

Suffragettes march for the right to vote, New York City, May 6, 1912.

But it may well admit of doubt whether, in the case of any race, an appointment of one of their number to a local office in a community in which the race feeling is so widespread and acute as to interfere with the ease and facility with which the local government business can be done by the appointee is of sufficient benefit by way of encouragement to the race to outweigh the recurrence and increase of race feeling which such an appointment is likely to engender. Therefore the Executive, in recognizing the Negro race by appointments, must exercise a careful discretion not thereby to do it more harm than good. On the other hand, we must be careful not to encourage the mere pretense of race feeling manufactured in the interest of individual political ambition.

Personally, I have not the slightest race prejudice or feeling, and recognition of its existence only awakens in my heart a deeper sympathy for those who have to bear it or suffer from it, and I question the wisdom of a policy which is likely to increase it. Meantime, if nothing is done to prevent it, a better feeling between the Negroes and the whites in the South will continue to grow, and more and more of the white people will come to realize that the future of the South is to be much benefited by the industrial and intellectual progress of the Negro. The exercise of political franchises by those of this race who are intelligent and well to do will be acquiesced in, and the right to vote will be withheld only from the ignorant and irresponsible of both races.

There is one other matter to which I shall refer. It was made the subject of great controversy during the election and calls for at least a passing reference now. My distinguished predecessor has given much attention to the cause of labor, with whose struggle for better things he has shown the sincerest sympathy. At his instance Congress has passed the bill fixing the liability of interstate carriers to their employees for injury sustained in the course of employment, abolishing the rule of fellow-servant and the common-law rule as to contributory negligence, and substituting therefor the so-called rule of "comparative negligence." It has also passed a law fixing the compensation of government employees for injuries sustained in the employ of the government through the negligence of the superior. It has also passed model child-labor law for the District of Columbia. In previous administrations an arbitration law for interstate commerce railroads and their employees, and laws for the application of safety devices to save the lives and limbs of employees of interstate railroads had been passed. Additional legislation of this kind was passed by the outgoing Congress.

I wish to say that insofar as I can I hope to promote the enactment of further legislation of this character. I am strongly convinced that the government should make itself as responsible to employees injured in its employ as an interstate-railway corporation is made responsible by federal law to its employees; and I shall be glad, whenever any additional reasonable safety device can be invented to reduce the loss of life and limb among railway employees, to urge Congress to require its adoption by interstate railways.

Another labor question has arisen which has awakened the most excited discussion. That is in respect to the power of the federal courts to issue injunctions in industrial disputes. As to that, my convictions are fixed. Take away from the courts, if it could be taken away, the power to issue injunctions in labor disputes, and it would create a privileged class among the laborers and save the lawless among their number from a most needful remedy available to all men for the protection of their business against lawless invasion. The proposition that business is not a property or pecuniary right which can be protected by equitable injunction is utterly without foundation in precedent or reason. The proposition is usually linked with one to make the secondary boycott lawful. Such a proposition is at variance with the American instinct, and will find no support, in my judgment, when submitted to the American people. The secondary boycott is an instrument of tyranny, and ought not to be made legitimate.

The issue of a temporary restraining order without notice has in several instances been abused by its inconsiderate exercise, and to remedy this the platform upon which I was elected recommends the formulation in a statute of the conditions under which such a temporary restraining order ought to issue. A statute can and ought to be framed to embody the best modern practice, and can bring the subject so closely to the attention of the court as to make abuses of the process unlikely in the future. The American people, if I understand them, insist that the authority of the courts shall be sustained, and are opposed to any change in the procedure by which the powers of a court may be weakened and the fearless and effective administration of justice be interfered with.

Having thus reviewed the questions likely to recur during my administration, and having expressed in a summary way the position which I expect to take in recommendations to Congress and in my conduct as an Executive, I invoke the considerate sympathy and support of my fellow citizens and the aid of the Almighty God in the discharge of my responsible duties.

Woodrow Wilson

28th President of the United States
1913–21

(Thomas) Woodrow Wilson

BORN: December 28, 1856, Staunton, Va.
MARRIED: Ellen Louise Axson, June 24, 1885; three
children; died August 6, 1914. Edith Bolling Galt,
December 18, 1915
DIED: February 3, 1924, Washington, D.C.
PARTY: Democratic
EDUCATION: Charles Hayward Barnwell School,
Columbia, Ga.; Davidson College (1873); College of
New Jersey (Princeton) (1879); University of Virginia
Law School (1889–90); Johns Hopkins University
(Ph.D. in political science, 1886).

CAREER:
Lawyer in Atlanta; professor, political economy and history at Bryn Mawr College (1885–88), Wesleyan University—where also football coach (1888–90), Princeton
University (1890–1902); president of Princeton
(1902–10); New Jersey governor (1911–13); president
(1913–21); Nobel Peace Prize (1919); retired in ill health.

PRESIDENTIAL CAMPAIGNS:
1912: Triumphed in his race against Republican incumbent Taft, Progressive Theodore Roosevelt, and Socialist
Eugene V. Debs.
1916: Reelected by a narrow margin in contest with
Republican Charles Evans Hughes, an associate justice,
U.S. Supreme Court.

As Europe's war threatens to spread, President Wilson marches in a "preparedness parade" in Washington, D.C., June 14, 1916.

Introduction

Woodrow Wilson was a brilliantly polished public speaker. His presentation is an inspired lecture by a luminous teacher whose style was strongly influenced by his father's great talent as a preaching minister. His confidence hardly reveals that he had been nominated only on the forty-sixth ballot at the Democrats' convention in Baltimore.

The address reflects the tenor of Wilson's multiparty campaign in 1912, primarily a contest between Theodore Roosevelt's preachment of New Nationalism and Wilson's call for New Freedom. Roosevelt advocated social planning by the federal government to achieve prosperity and happiness for the American people. Wilson argued for protecting people in small businesses. While he knew that the formidable trusts could not be eliminated, he stood against "the curse of bigness" in commerce.

On his way to Washington, Wilson expressed the thought that it would be "an irony of fate" if his administration were to be concerned with foreign affairs. Yet the address contained not a single reference to the subject. He was certain that he was engaged above all in starting a national crusade to remake and uplift domestic life and his speech was a plea for service in that undertaking.

Wilson was so serious that he did not arrange inaugural parties, although he did join the celebratory dinner held by his Princeton classmates.

Woodrow Wilson
First Inaugural Address
Tuesday, March 4, 1913

There has been a change of government. It began two years ago, when the House of Representatives became Democratic by a decisive majority. It has now been completed. The Senate about to assemble will also be Democratic. The offices of president and vice president have been put into the hands of Democrats. What does the change mean? That is the question that is uppermost in our minds today. That is the question I am going to try to answer, in order, if I may, to interpret the occasion.

It means much more than the mere success of a party. The success of a party means little except when the nation is using that party for a large and definite purpose. No one can mistake the purpose for which the nation now seeks to use the Democratic Party. It seeks to use it to interpret a change in its own plans and point of view. Some old things with which we had grown familiar, and which had begun to creep into the very habit of our thought and of our lives, have altered their aspect as we have latterly looked critically upon them, with fresh, awakened eyes; have dropped their disguises and shown themselves alien and sinister. Some new things, as we look frankly upon them, willing to comprehend their real character, have come to assume the aspect of things long believed in and familiar, stuff of our own convictions. We have been refreshed by a new insight into our own life.

We see that in many things that life is very great. It is incomparably great in its material aspects, in its body of wealth, in the diversity and sweep of its energy, in the industries which have been conceived and built up by the genius of individual men and the limitless enterprise of groups of men. It is great, also, very great, in its moral force. Nowhere else in the world have noble men and women exhibited in more striking forms the beauty and the energy of sympathy and helpfulness and counsel in their efforts to rectify wrong, alleviate suffering, and set the weak in the way of strength and hope. We have built up, moreover, a great system of government, which has stood through a long age as in many respects a model for those who seek to set liberty upon foundations that will endure against fortuitous change, against storm and accident. Our life contains every great thing, and contains it in rich abundance.

But the evil has come with the good, and much fine gold has been corroded. With riches has come inexcusable waste. We have squandered a great part of what we might have used, and have not stopped to conserve the exceeding bounty of nature, without which our genius for enterprise would have been worthless and impotent, scorning to be careful, shamefully prodigal as well as admirably efficient. We have been proud of our industrial achievements, but we have not hitherto stopped thoughtfully enough to count the human cost, the cost of lives snuffed out, of energies overtaxed and broken, the fearful physical and spiritual cost to the men and women and children upon whom the dead weight and burden of it all has fallen pitilessly the years through. The groans and agony of it all had not yet reached our ears, the solemn, moving undertone of our life, coming up out of the mines and factories, and out of every home where the struggle had its intimate and familiar seat. With the great government went many deep secret things which we too long delayed to look into and scrutinize with candid, fearless eyes. The great government we loved has too often been made use of for private and selfish purposes, and those who used it had forgotten the people.

At last a vision has been vouchsafed us of our life as a whole. We see the bad with the good, the debased and decadent with the sound and vital. With this vision we approach new affairs. Our duty is to cleanse, to reconsider, to restore, to correct the evil without impairing the good, to purify and humanize every process of our common life without weakening or sentimentalizing it. There has been something crude and heartless and unfeeling in our haste to succeed and be great. Our thought has been "Let every man look out for himself, let every generation look out for itself," while we reared giant machinery which made it impossible that any but those who stood at the levers of control should have a chance to look out for themselves. We had not forgotten our morals. We remembered well enough that we had set up a policy which was meant to serve the humblest as well as the most powerful, with an eye single to the standards of justice and fair play, and remembered it with pride. But we were very heedless and in a hurry to be great.

We have come now to the sober second thought. The scales of heedlessness have fallen from our eyes. We have made up our minds to square every process of our national life again with the standards we so proudly set up at the beginning and have always carried at our hearts. Our work is a work of restoration.

We have itemized with some degree of particularity the things that ought to be altered and here are some of the chief items: A tariff which cuts us off from our proper part in the commerce of the world, violates the just principles of taxation, and makes the government a facile instrument in the hand of private interests; a banking and currency system based upon the necessity of the government to sell its bonds fifty years ago and perfectly adapted to concentrating cash and restricting credits; an industrial system which, take it on all its sides, financial as well as administrative, holds capital in leading strings, restricts the liberties and limits the opportunities of labor, and exploits without renewing or conserving the natural resources of the country; a body of agricultural activities never yet given the efficiency of great business undertakings or served as it should be through the instrumentality of science taken directly to the farm, or afforded the facilities of credit best suited to its practical needs; watercourses undeveloped, waste places unreclaimed, forests untended, fast disappearing without plan or prospect of renewal, unregarded waste heaps at every mine. We have studied as perhaps no other nation has the most effective means of production, but we have not studied cost or economy as we should either as organizers of industry, as statesmen, or as individuals.

Nor have we studied and perfected the means by which government may be put at the service of humanity, in safeguarding the health of the nation, the health of its men and its women and its children, as well as their rights in the struggle for existence. This is no sentimental duty. The firm basis of government is justice, not pity. These are matters of justice. There can be no equality of opportunity, the first essential of justice in the body politic, if men and women and children be not shielded in their lives, their very vitality, from the consequences of great industrial and social processes which they can

43

not alter, control, or singly cope with. Society must see to it that it does not itself crush or weaken or damage its own constituent parts. The first duty of law is to keep sound the society it serves. Sanitary laws, pure food laws, and laws determining conditions of labor which individuals are powerless to determine for themselves are intimate parts of the very business of justice and legal efficiency.

These are some of the things we ought to do, and not leave the others undone, the old-fashioned, never-to-be-neglected, fundamental safeguarding of property and of individual right. This is the high enterprise of the new day: To lift everything that concerns our life as a nation to the light that shines from the hearthfire of every man's conscience and vision of the right. It is inconceivable that we should do this as partisans; it is inconceivable we should do it in ignorance of the facts as they are or in blind haste. We shall restore, not destroy. We shall deal with our economic system as it is and as it may be modified, not as it might be if we had a clean sheet of paper to write upon; and step by step we shall make it what it should be, in the spirit of those who question their own wisdom and seek counsel and knowledge, not shallow self-satisfaction or the excitement of excursions whither they can not tell. Justice, and only justice, shall always be our motto.

And yet it will be no cool process of mere science. The nation has been deeply stirred, stirred by a solemn passion, stirred by the knowledge of wrong, of ideals lost, of government too often debauched and made an instrument of evil. The feelings with which we face this new age of right and opportunity sweep across our heartstrings like some air out of God's own presence, where justice and mercy are reconciled and the judge and the brother are one. We know our task to be no mere task of politics but a task which shall search us through and through, whether we be able to understand our time and the need of our people, whether we be indeed their spokesmen and interpreters, whether we have the pure heart to comprehend and the rectified will to choose our high course of action.

This is not a day of triumph; it is a day of dedication. Here muster, not the forces of party, but the forces of humanity. Men's hearts wait upon us; men's lives hang in the balance; men's hopes call upon us to say what we will do. Who shall live up to the great trust? Who dares fail to try? I summon all honest men, all patriotic, all forward-looking men, to my side. God helping me, I will not fail them, if they will but counsel and sustain me!

INTRODUCTION

When the World War began early in his first term, the president urged Americans "to be neutral in fact as well as in name . . . impartial in thought as well as in action." Public opinion and his own private view favored Britain and France battling the aggressive military might of Germany, the leader of the Central Powers. But running for reelection in 1916, Wilson's winning slogan was "He kept us out of war."

Still, German submarines were sinking supply ships, neutral as well as enemy, meaning American vessels and citizens were in constant danger. Germany, which had pledged not to sink unarmed ships without warning, announced just a few weeks before Wilson's second inauguration that it intended to resume "unrestricted submarine warfare." Wilson's mind consequently was now on waging war, not on remaining neutral. Only one month later, on April 6, the United States did declare war on Germany.

This address, thrown together quickly, did not rise to Wilson's usual rhetorical standard. He began with a brief salute to the progressive legislation Congress had enacted and went on to the real burden of his thinking: The nation could soon be in the fighting. He put it artfully: We may be "drawn on . . . to a more active assertion of our rights as we see them and a more immediate association with the great struggle itself."

Woodrow Wilson
Second Inaugural Address
Monday, March 5, 1917

My Fellow Citizens:

The four years which have elapsed since last I stood in this place have been crowded with counsel and action of the most vital interest and consequence. Perhaps no equal period in our history has been so fruitful of important reforms in our economic and industrial life or so full of significant changes in the spirit and purpose of our political action. We have sought very thoughtfully to set our house in order, correct the grosser errors and abuses of our industrial life, liberate and quicken the processes of our national genius and energy, and lift our politics to a broader view of the people's essential interests.

It is a record of singular variety and singular distinction. But I shall not attempt to review it. It speaks for itself and will be of increasing influence as the years go by. This is not the time for retrospect. It is time rather to speak our thoughts and purposes concerning the present and the immediate future.

Although we have centered counsel and action with such unusual concentration and success upon the great problems of domestic legislation to which we addressed ourselves four years ago, other matters have more and more forced themselves upon our attention—matters lying outside our own life as a nation and over which we had no control, but which, despite our wish to keep free of them, have drawn us more and more irresistibly into their own current and influence.

It has been impossible to avoid them. They have affected the life of the whole world. They have shaken men everywhere with a passion and an apprehension they never knew before. It has been hard to preserve calm counsel while the thought of our own people swayed this way and that under their influence. We are a composite and cosmopolitan people. We are of the blood of all the nations that are at war.[1] The currents of our thoughts as well as the currents of our trade run quick at all seasons back and forth between us and them. The war inevitably set its mark from the first alike upon our minds, our industries, our commerce, our politics and our social action. To be indifferent to it, or independent of it, was out of the question.

And yet all the while we have been conscious that we were not part of it. In that consciousness, despite many divisions, we have drawn closer together. We have been deeply wronged upon the

---

1. The Great War (later renamed World War I), 1914–18, broke out in Europe in August 1914 and quickly engulfed many of the countries from which Americans had emigrated. The United States remained neutral through Wilson's first term but declared war on Germany on April 6, 1917, a month after this address.

U.S. Army gun crew advances against German trenches, 1918.

seas,[2] but we have not wished to wrong or injure in return; have retained throughout the consciousness of standing in some sort apart, intent upon an interest that transcended the immediate issues of the war itself.

As some of the injuries done us have become intolerable we have still been clear that we wished nothing for ourselves that we were not ready to demand for all mankind—fair dealing, justice, the freedom to live and to be at ease against organized wrong.

It is in this spirit and with this thought that we have grown more and more aware, more and more certain that the part we wished to play was the part of those who mean to vindicate and fortify peace. We have been obliged to arm ourselves to make good our claim to a certain minimum of right and of freedom of action. We stand firm in armed neutrality since it seems that in no other way we can demonstrate what it is we insist upon and cannot forget. We may even be drawn on, by circumstances, not by our own purpose or desire, to a more active assertion of our rights as we see them and a more immediate association with the great struggle itself. But nothing will alter our thought or our purpose. They are too clear to be obscured.

---

2. On January 31, 1917, Germany had announced unrestricted submarine warfare, and on February 3 the United States severed relations with Germany.

They are too deeply rooted in the principles of our national life to be altered. We desire neither conquest nor advantage. We wish nothing that can be had only at the cost of another people. We always professed unselfish purpose and we covet the opportunity to prove our professions are sincere.

There are many things still to be done at home, to clarify our own politics and add new vitality to the industrial processes of our own life, and we shall do them as time and opportunity serve, but we realize that the greatest things that remain to be done must be done with the whole world for stage and in cooperation with the wide and universal forces of mankind, and we are making our spirits ready for those things.

We are provincials no longer. The tragic events of the thirty months of vital turmoil through which we have just passed have made us citizens of the world. There can be no turning back. Our own fortunes as a nation are involved whether we would have it so or not.

And yet we are not the less Americans on that account. We shall be the more American if we but remain true to the principles in which we have been bred. They are not the principles of a province or of a single continent. We have known and boasted all along that they were the principles of a liberated mankind. These, therefore, are the things we shall stand for, whether in war or in peace:

That all nations are equally interested in the peace of the world and in the political stability of free peoples, and equally responsible for their maintenance; that the essential principle of peace is the actual equality of nations in all matters of right or privilege; that peace cannot securely or justly rest upon an armed balance of power; that governments derive all their just powers from the consent of the governed and that no other powers should be supported by the common thought, purpose or power of the family of nations; that the seas should be equally free and safe for the use of all peoples, under rules set up by common agreement and consent, and that, so far as practicable, they should be accessible to all upon equal terms; that national armaments shall be limited to the necessities of national order and domestic safety; that the community of interest and of power upon which peace must henceforth depend imposes upon each nation the duty of seeing to it that all influences proceeding from its own citizens meant to encourage or assist revolution in other states should be sternly and effectually suppressed and prevented.

I need not argue these principles to you, my fellow countrymen; they are your own part and parcel of your own thinking and your own motives in affairs. They spring up native amongst us. Upon this as a platform of purpose and of action we can stand together. And it is imperative that we should

The Signing of Peace in the Hall of Mirrors, Versailles *(France)* 28th June, 1919; *oil painting by Sir William Orpen. President Wilson sits slightly left of center, French Premier Clemenceau to his right, German delegates across the table.*

stand together. We are being forged into a new unity amidst the fires that now blaze throughout the world. In their ardent heat we shall, in God's Providence, let us hope, be purged of faction and division, purified of the errant humors of party and of private interest, and shall stand forth in the days to come with a new dignity of national pride and spirit. Let each man see to it that the dedication is in his own heart, the high purpose of the nation in his own mind, ruler of his own will and desire.

I stand here and have taken the high and solemn oath to which you have been audience because the people of the United States have chosen me for this august delegation of power and have by their gracious judgment named me their leader in affairs.

I know now what the task means. I realize to the full the responsibility which it involves. I pray God I may be given the wisdom and the prudence to do my duty in the true spirit of this great people. I am their servant and can succeed only as they sustain and guide me by their confidence and their counsel. The thing I shall count upon, the thing without which neither counsel nor action will avail, is the unity of America—an America united in feeling, in purpose and in its vision of duty, of opportunity and of service.

We are to beware of all men who would turn the tasks and the necessities of the nation to their own private profit or use them for the building up of private power.

United alike in the conception of our duty and in the high resolve to perform it in the face of all men, let us dedicate ourselves to the great task to which we must now set our hand. For myself I beg your tolerance, your countenance and your united aid.

The shadows that now lie dark upon our path will soon be dispelled, and we shall walk with the light all about us if we be but true to ourselves—to ourselves as we have wished to be known in the counsels of the world and in the thought of all those who love liberty and justice and the right exalted.

Warren Gamaliel Harding

29th President of the United States
1921–23

Warren Gamaliel Harding

BORN: November 2, 1865, Blooming Grove, Ohio
MARRIED: Florence Kling De Wolfe, July 8, 1891; one child, out of wedlock
DIED: August 2, 1923, San Francisco, Calif.
PARTY: Republican
EDUCATION: Public schools in Marion; Ohio Central College (1882); studied law briefly.

CAREER:
School teacher; insurance business; editor and publisher of the *Marion Star;* Ohio State Senate (1899–1903); Ohio lieutenant governor (1904–05); unsuccessful bid for governor (1910); U.S. Senate (1915–21); president (1921–23); died in office.

PRESIDENTIAL CAMPAIGN:
1920: Chosen to head the Republican ticket although not a national figure. After an initial "front porch" campaign—such as William McKinley, a fellow Ohioan he immensely admired, ran in 1896—he switched tactics, delivered 112 campaign speeches in various parts of the country, and became a major Republican voice. The first presidential returns ever reported on radio showed him crushing Democrat James M. Cox, another Ohio newspaper publisher.

President Harding and his wife, Florence, October 5, 1920.

INTRODUCTION

Warren Harding has been considered one of the worst American presidents because of the scandals that broke out in his administration, although a recent biography has considerably raised his reputation.

Harding's speeches, often rambling, were described by one critic as consisting of "an army of pompous phrases moving over the landscape in search of an idea." He often talked of returning the country to "normalcy," a word he brought into vogue to describe what he regarded as the simpler pre-World War society. Still, like a modern man, he rode with Wilson to his inauguration in an automobile, the first time a president-elect had not arrived for his swearing-in by horse-drawn carriage. Moreover, his verbose inaugural was the first ever described on the radio and the first heard over a loudspeaker by the crowd in the stands.

In the address, he satisfied many Republicans by not saying the country should join the League of Nations, but he blurred his position on the subject by his endorsement of "an association of nations." He was for a protective tariff and he denounced revolution— such as had recently occurred in Russia. His many very stretched sentences make the inaugural read better than it sounded upon delivery.

Warren Gamaliel Harding
Inaugural Address

Friday, March 4, 1921

My Countrymen:

When one surveys the world about him after the great storm, noting the marks of destruction and yet rejoicing in the ruggedness of the things which withstood it, if he is an American he breathes the clarified atmosphere with a strange mingling of regret and new hope. We have seen a world passion spend its fury, but we contemplate our Republic unshaken, and hold our civilization secure. Liberty—liberty within the law—and civilization are inseparable, and though both were threatened we find them now secure; and there comes to Americans the profound assurance that our representative government is the highest expression and surest guaranty of both.

Standing in this presence, mindful of the solemnity of this occasion, feeling the emotions which no one may know until he senses the great weight of responsibility for himself, I must utter my belief in the divine inspiration of the founding fathers. Surely there must have been God's intent in the making of this new-world republic. Ours is an organic law which had but one ambiguity,[1] and we saw that effaced in a baptism of sacrifice and blood, with union maintained, the nation supreme, and its concord inspiring. We have seen the world rivet its hopeful gaze on the great truths on which the founders wrought. We have seen civil, human, and religious liberty verified and glorified. In the beginning the Old World scoffed at our experiment; today our foundations of political and social belief stand unshaken, a precious inheritance to ourselves, an inspiring example of freedom and civilization to all mankind. Let us express renewed and strengthened devotion, in grateful reverence for the immortal beginning, and utter our confidence in the supreme fulfillment.

The recorded progress of our republic, materially and spiritually, in itself proves the wisdom of the inherited policy of noninvolvement in Old World affairs. Confident of our ability to work out our own destiny, and jealously guarding our right to do so, we seek no part in directing the destinies of the Old World. We do not mean to be entangled. We will accept no responsibility except as our own conscience and judgment, in each instance, may determine.

Our eyes never will be blind to a developing menace, our ears never deaf to the call of civiliza-

---

1. Harding is referring to the condoning of slavery by the U.S. Constitution, as well as to the Civil War, which preserved the Union and led to emancipation.

tion. We recognize the new order in the world, with the closer contacts which progress has wrought. We sense the call of the human heart for fellowship, fraternity, and cooperation. We crave friendship and harbor no hate. But America, our America, the America builded on the foundation laid by the inspired fathers, can be a party to no permanent military alliance. It can enter into no political commitments, nor assume any economic obligations which will subject our decisions to any other than our own authority.

I am sure our own people will not misunderstand, nor will the world misconstrue. We have no thought to impede the paths to closer relationship. We wish to promote understanding. We want to do our part in making offensive warfare so hateful that governments and peoples who resort to it must prove the righteousness of their cause or stand as outlaws before the bar of civilization.

We are ready to associate ourselves with the nations of the world, great and small, for conference, for counsel; to seek the expressed views of world opinion; to recommend a way to approximate disarmament and relieve the crushing burdens of military and naval establishments. We elect to participate in suggesting plans for mediation, conciliation, and arbitration, and would gladly join in that expressed conscience of progress, which seeks to clarify and write the laws of international relationship, and establish a world court for the disposition of such justiciable questions as nations are agreed to submit thereto. In expressing aspirations, in seeking practical plans, in translating humanity's new concept of righteousness and justice and its hatred of war into recommended action we are ready most heartily to unite, but every commitment must be made in the exercise of our national sovereignty. Since freedom impelled, and independence inspired, and nationality exalted, a world supergovernment is contrary to everything we cherish and can have no sanction by our Republic. This is not selfishness, it is sanctity. It is not aloofness, it is security. It is not suspicion of others, it is patriotic adherence to the things which made us what we are.

Today, better than ever before, we know the aspirations of humankind, and share them. We have come to a new realization of our place in the world and a new appraisal of our nation by the world. The unselfishness of these United States is a thing proven; our devotion to peace for ourselves and for the world is well established; our concern for preserved civilization has had its impassioned and heroic expression. There was no American failure to resist the attempted reversion of civilization; there will be no failure today or tomorrow.

The success of our popular government rests wholly upon the correct interpretation of the deliberate, intelligent, dependable popular will of America. In a deliberate questioning of a suggested change of national policy, where internationality was to supersede nationality, we turned to a referendum, to the American people. There was ample discussion, and there is a public mandate in manifest understanding.

America is ready to encourage, eager to initiate, anxious to participate in any seemly program likely to lessen the probability of war, and promote that brotherhood of mankind which must be God's highest conception of human relationship. Because we cherish ideals of justice and peace, because we appraise international comity and helpful relationship no less highly than any people of the world, we aspire to a high place in the moral leadership of civilization, and we hold a maintained America, the proven republic, the unshaken temple of representative democracy, to be not only an inspiration and example, but the highest agency of strengthening good will and promoting accord on both continents.

Mankind needs a worldwide benediction of understanding. It is needed among individuals, among peoples, among governments, and it will inaugurate an era of good feeling to make the birth of a new order. In such understanding men will strive confidently for the promotion of their better relationships and nations will promote the comities so essential to peace.

We must understand that ties of trade bind

nations in closest intimacy, and none may receive except as he gives. We have not strengthened ours in accordance with our resources or our genius, notably on our own continent, where a galaxy of republics reflects the glory of new-world democracy, but in the new order of finance and trade we mean to promote enlarged activities and seek expanded confidence.

Perhaps we can make no more helpful contribution by example than prove a republic's capacity to emerge from the wreckage of war. While the world's embittered travail did not leave us devastated lands nor desolated cities, left no gaping wounds, no breast with hate, it did involve us in the delirium of expenditure, in expanded currency and credits, in unbalanced industry, in unspeakable waste, and disturbed relationships. While it uncovered our portion of hateful selfishness at home, it also revealed the heart of America as sound and fearless, and beating in confidence unfailing.

Amid it all we have riveted the gaze of all civilization to the unselfishness and the righteousness of representative democracy, where our freedom never has made offensive warfare, never has sought territorial aggrandizement through force, never has turned to the arbitrament of arms until reason has been exhausted. When the governments of the earth shall have established a freedom like our own and shall have sanctioned the pursuit of peace as we have practiced it, I believe the last sorrow and the final sacrifice of international warfare will have been written.

Let me speak to the maimed and wounded soldiers who are present today, and through them convey to their comrades the gratitude of the Republic for their sacrifices in its defense. A generous country will never forget the services you rendered, and you may hope for a policy under government that will relieve any maimed successors from taking your places on another such occasion as this.

Our supreme task is the resumption of our onward, normal way. Reconstruction, readjustment, restoration all these must follow. I would like to hasten them. If it will lighten the spirit and add to the resolution with which we take up the task, let me repeat for our nation, we shall give no people just cause to make war upon us; we hold no national prejudices; we entertain no spirit of revenge; we do not hate; we do not covet; we dream of no conquest, nor boast of armed prowess.

If, despite this attitude, war is again forced upon us, I earnestly hope a way may be found which will unify our individual and collective strength and consecrate all America, materially and spiritually, body and soul, to national defense. I can vision the ideal republic, where every man and woman is called under the flag for assignment to duty for whatever service, military or civic, the individual is best fitted; where we may call to universal service

JUGGERNAUT.

President Harding's administration was tarnished by bribery involving leasing of oil reserves at Teapot Dome, Wyoming. Cartoon by Clifford Berryman, 1924.

every plant, agency, or facility, all in the sublime sacrifice for country, and not one penny of war profit shall inure to the benefit of private individual, corporation, or combination, but all above the normal shall flow into the defense chest of the nation. There is something inherently wrong, something out of accord with the ideals of representative democracy, when one portion of our citizenship turns its activities to private gain amid defensive war while another is fighting, sacrificing, or dying for national preservation.

Out of such universal service will come a new unity of spirit and purpose, a new confidence and consecration, which would make our defense impregnable, our triumph assured. Then we should have little or no disorganization of our economic, industrial, and commercial systems at home, no staggering war debts, no swollen fortunes to flout the sacrifices of our soldiers, no excuse for sedition, no pitiable slackerism, no outrage of treason. Envy and jealousy would have no soil for their menacing development, and revolution would be without the passion which engenders it.

A regret for the mistakes of yesterday must not, however, blind us to the tasks of today. War never left such an aftermath. There has been staggering loss of life and measureless wastage of materials. Nations are still groping for return to stable ways. Discouraging indebtedness confronts us like all the war-torn nations, and these obligations must be provided for. No civilization can survive repudiation.

We can reduce the abnormal expenditures, and we will. We can strike at war taxation, and we must. We must face the grim necessity, with full knowledge that the task is to be solved, and we must proceed with a full realization that no statute enacted by man can repeal the inexorable laws of nature. Our most dangerous tendency is to expect too much of government, and at the same time do for it too little. We contemplate the immediate task of putting our public household in order. We need a rigid and yet sane economy, combined with fiscal justice, and it must be attended by individual prudence and thrift, which are so essential to this trying hour and reassuring for the future.

The business world reflects the disturbance of war's reaction. Herein flows the lifeblood of material existence. The economic mechanism is intricate and its parts interdependent, and has suffered the shocks and jars incident to abnormal demands, credit inflations, and price upheavals. The normal balances have been impaired, the channels of distribution have been clogged, the relations of labor and management have been strained. We must seek the readjustment with care and courage. Our people must give and take. Prices must reflect the receding fever of war activities. Perhaps we never shall know the old levels of wages again, because war invariably readjusts compensations, and the necessaries of life will show their inseparable relationship, but we must strive for normalcy to reach stability. All the penalties will not be light, nor evenly distributed. There is no way of making them so. There is no instant step from disorder to order. We must face a condition of grim reality, charge off our losses and start afresh. It is the oldest lesson of civilization. I would like government to do all it can to mitigate; then, in understanding, in mutuality of interest, in concern for the common good, our tasks will be solved. No altered system will work a miracle. Any wild experiment will only add to the confusion. Our best assurance lies in efficient administration of our proven system.

The forward course of the business cycle is unmistakable. Peoples are turning from destruction to production. Industry has sensed the changed order and our own people are turning to resume their normal, onward way. The call is for productive America to go on. I know that Congress and the Administration will favor every wise government policy to aid the resumption and encourage continued progress.

I speak for administrative efficiency, for lightened tax burdens, for sound commercial practices, for adequate credit facilities, for sympathetic concern for all agricultural problems, for the omission of unnecessary interference of government with business, for an end to government's experiment in business, and for more efficient business in government administration. With all of this must attend a mindfulness of the human side of all activities, so that social, industrial, and economic justice will be squared with the purposes of a righteous people.

With the nationwide induction of womanhood into our political life,[2] we may count upon her intuitions, her refinements, her intelligence, and her influence to exalt the social order. We count upon her exercise of the full privileges and the performance of the duties of citizenship to speed the attainment of the highest state.

I wish for an America no less alert in guarding against dangers from within than it is watchful against enemies from without. Our fundamental law recognizes no class, no group, no section; there must be none in legislation or administration. The supreme inspiration is the common weal. Humanity hungers for international peace, and we crave it with all mankind. My most reverent prayer for America is for industrial peace, with its rewards, widely and generally distributed, amid the inspirations of equal opportunity. No one justly may deny the equality of opportunity which made us what we are. We have

---

2. The Nineteenth Amendment to the U.S. Constitution, ensuring women's right to vote, had been ratified in August 1920, only a little more than six months before this address.

mistaken unpreparedness to embrace it to be a challenge of the reality, and due concern for making all citizens fit for participation will give added strength of citizenship and magnify our achievement.

If revolution[3] insists upon overturning established order, let other peoples make the tragic experiment. There is no place for it in America. When world war threatened civilization we pledged our resources and our lives to its preservation, and when revolution threatens we unfurl the flag of law and order and renew our consecration. Ours is a constitutional freedom where the popular will is the law supreme and minorities are sacredly protected. Our revisions, reformations, and evolutions reflect a deliberate judgment and an orderly progress, and we mean to cure our ills, but never destroy or permit destruction by force.

I had rather submit our industrial controversies to the conference table in advance than to a settlement table after conflict and suffering. The earth is thirsting for the cup of good will, understanding is its fountain source. I would like to acclaim an era of good feeling amid dependable prosperity and all the blessings which attend.

It has been proved again and again that we cannot, while throwing our markets open to the world, main-

---

3. Refers to the Russian Revolution (1917). Fighting and unrest continued in 1921.

tain American standards of living and opportunity, and hold our industrial eminence in such unequal competition. There is a luring fallacy in the theory of banished barriers of trade, but preserved American standards require our higher production costs to be reflected in our tariffs on imports. Today, as never before, when peoples are seeking trade restoration and expansion, we must adjust our tariffs to the new order. We seek participation in the world's exchanges, because therein lies our way to widened influence and the triumphs of peace. We know full well we cannot sell where we do not buy, and we cannot sell successfully where we do not carry. Opportunity is calling not alone for the restoration, but for a new era in production, transportation and trade. We shall answer it best by meeting the demand of a surpassing home market, by promoting self-reliance in production, and by bidding enterprise, genius, and efficiency to carry our cargoes in American bottoms to the marts of the world.

We would not have an America living within and for herself alone, but we would have her self-reliant, independent, and ever nobler, stronger, and richer. Believing in our higher standards, reared through constitutional liberty and maintained opportunity, we invite the world to the same heights. But pride in things wrought is no reflex of a completed task. Common welfare is the goal of our national endeavor. Wealth is not inimical to welfare; it ought to be its friendliest agency. There never can be equality of rewards or possessions so long as the human plan contains varied talents and differing degrees of industry and thrift, but ours ought to be a country free from the great blotches of distressed poverty. We ought to find a way to guard against the perils and penalties of unemployment. We want an America of homes, illumined with hope and happiness, where mothers, freed from the necessity for long hours of toil beyond their own doors, may preside as befits the hearthstone of American citizenship. We want the cradle of American childhood rocked under conditions so wholesome and so hopeful that no blight may touch it in its development, and we want to provide that no selfish interest, no material necessity, no lack of opportunity shall prevent the gaining of that education so essential to best citizenship.

There is no short cut to the making of these ideals into glad realities. The world has witnessed again and again the futility and the mischief of ill-considered remedies for social and economic disorders. But we are mindful today as never before of the friction of modern industrialism, and we must learn its causes and reduce its evil consequences by sober and tested methods. Where genius has made for great possibilities, justice and happiness must be reflected in a greater common welfare.

Service is the supreme commitment of life. I

would rejoice to acclaim the era of the Golden Rule and crown it with the autocracy of service. I pledge an administration wherein all the agencies of government are called to serve, and ever promote an understanding of government purely as an expression of the popular will.

One cannot stand in this presence and be unmindful of the tremendous responsibility. The world upheaval has added heavily to our tasks. But with the realization comes the surge of high resolve, and there is reassurance in belief in the God-given destiny of our republic. If I felt that there is to be sole responsibility in the Executive for the America of tomorrow I should shrink from the burden. But here are a hundred millions, with common concern and shared responsibility, answerable to God and country. The Republic summons them to their duty, and I invite cooperation.

I accept my part with single-mindedness of purpose and humility of spirit, and implore the favor and guidance of God in His Heaven. With these I am unafraid, and confidently face the future.

I have taken the solemn oath of office on that passage of Holy Writ wherein it is asked: "What doth the Lord require of thee but to do justly, and to love mercy, and to walk humbly with thy God?"[4] This I plight to God and country.

---

4. Micah 6:8.

Calvin Coolidge

30th President of the United States
1923–29

(John) Calvin Coolidge

BORN: July 4, 1872, Plymouth Notch, Vt.
MARRIED: Grace Anna Goodhue, October 4, 1905;
two children
DIED: January 5, 1933, Northampton, Mass.
PARTY: Republican
EDUCATION: Public school; Black River Academy;
St. Johnsbury Academy; Amherst College (cum laude
1895); studied law, Northampton, Mass. (1897).

CAREER:
Lawyer in Northampton; local government offices from
1899; Massachusetts General Court (1907–08);
Northampton mayor (1910–11); Massachusetts State
Senate (1912–15); Senate president (1915); lieutenant
governor (1916–18); governor (1919–20); vice president
(1921–23); president (1923–29); retired to Northampton.

PRESIDENTIAL CAMPAIGNS:
1923: Became president on Harding's sudden death.
1924: Ran with Charles G. Dawes of Illinois, first director of the Bureau of the Budget and a Nobel Peace Prize
laureate, against Democrat John W. Davis of West Virginia, Solicitor General under President Wilson, and
Progressive Senator Robert M. La Follette of Wiscon-
sin; received 54 percent of popular vote.
1928: Chose not to run.

President Coolidge, Vice President Dawes and their wives
watch the inaugural parade from a reviewing stand
in front of the White House, March 4, 1925.

Introduction

Calvin Coolidge became president on Harding's death in 1923. He had been chosen in 1920 to be vice president after emerging as a popular national figure when, in 1919, as governor of Massachusetts, he called out troops to deal with a Boston police strike.

After taking the presidential oath of office by a kerosene lamp while his father, a storekeeper in Vermont, held the Bible, he was asked about his feelings on reaching the presidency so unexpectedly. He replied, "I thought I could swing it." Coolidge, a stern and cold personality with a facial expression described as vinegary, would afterwards say that the presidency was "like the glory of the morning sunrise."

But Coolidge brought to his inauguration immense sadness. His younger son, Calvin, had died the previous year of blood-poisoning caused by an infected blister on his foot. Coolidge later would write: "When he went, the power and the glory of the presidency went with it . . . . I don't know why such a price is exacted for occupying the White House."

His oath-taking and address were carried over radio, providing a new experience to an audience estimated at 25 million people. The uninspiring speech that took forty-two minutes to deliver deals optimistically with issues of the day, including peace and disarmament and his support of America's joining a world court.

Calvin Coolidge
Inaugural Address
Wednesday, March 4, 1925

My Countrymen:
No one can contemplate current conditions without finding much that is satisfying and still more that is encouraging. Our own country is leading the world in the general readjustment to the results of the great conflict. Many of its burdens will bear heavily upon us for years, and the secondary and indirect effects we must expect to experience for some time. But we are beginning to comprehend more definitely what course should be pursued, what remedies ought to be applied, what actions should be taken for our deliverance, and are clearly manifesting a determined will faithfully and conscientiously to adopt these methods of relief. Already we have sufficiently rearranged our domestic affairs so that confidence has returned, business has revived, and we appear to be entering an era of prosperity which is gradually reaching into every part of the nation. Realizing that we can not live unto ourselves alone, we have contributed of our resources and our counsel to the relief of the suffering and the settlement of the disputes among the European nations. Because of what America is and what America has done, a

firmer courage, a higher hope, inspires the heart of all humanity.

These results have not occurred by mere chance. They have been secured by a constant and enlightened effort marked by many sacrifices and extending over many generations. We can not continue these brilliant successes in the future, unless we continue to learn from the past. It is necessary to keep the former experiences of our country both at home and abroad continually before us, if we are to have any science of government. If we wish to erect new structures, we must have a definite knowledge of the old foundations. We must realize that human nature is about the most constant thing in the universe and that the essentials of human relationship do not change. We must frequently take our bearings from these fixed stars of our political firmament if we expect to hold a true course. If we examine carefully what we have done, we can determine the more accurately what we can do.

We stand at the opening of the one hundred and fiftieth year since our national consciousness first asserted itself by unmistakable action with an array of force.[1] The old sentiment of detached and dependent colonies disappeared in the new sentiment of a united and independent nation. Men began to discard the narrow confines of a local charter for the broader

---

1. Refers to the Declaration of Independence, 1776.

opportunities of a national constitution. Under the eternal urge of freedom we became an independent Nation. A little less than fifty years later that freedom and independence were reasserted in the face of all the world, and guarded, supported, and secured by the Monroe doctrine.[2] The narrow fringe of states along the Atlantic seaboard advanced its frontiers across the hills and plains of an intervening continent until it passed down the golden slope to the Pacific. We made freedom a birthright. We extended our domain over distant islands[3] in order to safeguard our own interests and accepted the consequent obligation to bestow justice and liberty upon less favored peoples. In the defense of our own ideals and in the general cause of liberty we entered the Great War. When victory had been fully secured, we withdrew to our own shores unrecompensed save in the consciousness of duty done.

Throughout all these experiences we have enlarged our freedom, we have strengthened our independence. We have been, and propose to be, more and more American. We believe that we can best serve our own country and most successfully discharge our obligations to humanity by continuing to be openly and candidly, intensely and

---

2. See note 4 in Taft address, page 14.
3. The United States acquired Puerto Rico, Guam, and the Philippines in the Treaty of Paris (1898), which ended the Spanish-American War.

scrupulously, American. If we have any heritage, it has been that. If we have any destiny, we have found it in that direction.

But if we wish to continue to be distinctively American, we must continue to make that term comprehensive enough to embrace the legitimate desires of a civilized and enlightened people determined in all their relations to pursue a conscientious and religious life. We can not permit ourselves to be narrowed and dwarfed by slogans and phrases. It is not the adjective, but the substantive, which is of real importance. It is not the name of the action, but the result of the action, which is the chief concern. It will be well not to be too much disturbed by the thought of either isolation or entanglement of pacifists and militarists. The physical configuration of the earth has separated us from all of the Old World, but the common brotherhood of man, the highest law of all our being, has united us by inseparable bonds with all humanity. Our country represents nothing but peaceful intentions toward all the earth, but it ought not to fail to maintain such a military force as comports with the dignity and security of a great people. It ought to be a balanced force, intensely modern, capable of defense by sea and land, beneath the surface and in the air. But it should be so conducted that all the world may see in it, not a menace, but an instrument of security and peace.

84

This nation believes thoroughly in an honorable peace under which the rights of its citizens are to be everywhere protected. It has never found that the necessary enjoyment of such a peace could be maintained only by a great and threatening array of arms. In common with other nations, it is now more determined than ever to promote peace through friendliness and good will, through mutual understandings and mutual forbearance. We have never practiced the policy of competitive armaments. We have recently committed ourselves by covenants with the other great nations to a limitation of our sea power.[4] As one result of this, our navy ranks larger, in comparison, than it ever did before. Removing the burden of expense and jealousy, which must always accrue from a keen rivalry, is one of the most effective methods of diminishing that unreasonable hysteria and misunderstanding which are the most potent means of fomenting war. This policy represents a new departure in the world. It is a thought, an ideal, which has led to an entirely new line of action. It will not be easy to maintain. Some never moved from their old positions, some are constantly slipping back to the old ways of thought and the old action of seizing a musket and

---

4. International Conference on Naval Limitation (1921–22), commonly known as The Washington Conference, resulted in treaties involving the United States, Japan, and various European countries on the use of sea power.

relying on force. America has taken the lead in this new direction, and that lead America must continue to hold. If we expect others to rely on our fairness and justice we must show that we rely on their fairness and justice.

If we are to judge by past experience, there is much to be hoped for in international relations from frequent conferences and consultations. We have before us the beneficial results of the Washington conference and the various consultations recently held upon European affairs, some of which were in response to our suggestions and in some of which we were active participants. Even the failures can not but be accounted useful and an immeasurable advance over threatened or actual warfare. I am strongly in favor of continuation of this policy, whenever conditions are such that there is even a promise that practical and favorable results might be secured.

In conformity with the principle that a display of reason rather than a threat of force should be the determining factor in the intercourse among nations, we have long advocated the peaceful settlement of disputes by methods of arbitration and have negotiated many treaties to secure that result. The same considerations should lead to our adherence to the Permanent Court of International Justice. Where great principles are involved, where great movements are under way which promise much for

Coolidge is sworn in by his father, a notary, in Vermont after Pres. Harding's death, 1923.

the welfare of humanity by reason of the very fact that many other nations have given such movements their actual support, we ought not to withhold our own sanction because of any small and inessential difference, but only upon the ground of the most important and compelling fundamental reasons. We can not barter away our independence or our sovereignty, but we ought to engage in no refinements of logic, no sophistries, and no subterfuges, to argue away the undoubted duty of this country by reason of the might of its numbers, the power of its resources, and its position of leadership in the world, actively and comprehensively to signify its approval and to bear its full share of the responsibility of a candid and disinterested attempt at the establishment of a tribunal for the administration of even-handed justice between nation and nation. The weight of our enormous influence must be cast upon the side of a reign not of force but of law and trial, not by battle but by reason.

We have never any wish to interfere in the political conditions of any other countries. Especially are we determined not to become implicated in the political controversies of the Old World. With a great deal of hesitation, we have responded to appeals for help to maintain order, protect life and property, and establish responsible government in some of the small countries of the Western Hemisphere. Our private citizens have advanced large sums of money to assist in the necessary financing and relief of the Old World. We have not failed, nor shall we fail to respond, whenever necessary to mitigate human suffering and assist in the rehabilitation of distressed nations. These, too, are requirements which must be met by reason of our vast powers and the place we hold in the world.

Some of the best thought of mankind has long been seeking for a formula for permanent peace. Undoubtedly the clarification of the principles of international law would be helpful, and the efforts of scholars to prepare such a work for adoption by the various nations should have our sympathy and support. Much may be hoped for from the earnest studies of those who advocate the outlawing of aggressive war. But all these plans and preparations, these treaties and covenants, will not of themselves be adequate. One of the greatest dangers to peace lies in the economic pressure to which people find themselves subjected. One of the most practical things to be done in the world is to seek arrangements under which such pressure may be removed, so that opportunity may be renewed and hope may be revived. There must be some assurance that effort and endeavor will be followed by success and prosperity. In the making and financing of such adjustments there is not only an opportunity, but a real duty, for America to respond with her counsel and her resources. Conditions must be provided under which people can make a living and work out of their difficulties. But there is another element, more important than all, without which there can not be the slightest hope of a permanent peace. That element lies in the heart of humanity. Unless the desire for peace be cherished there, unless this fundamental and only natural source of brotherly love be cultivated to its highest degree, all artificial efforts will be in vain. Peace will come when there is realization that only under a reign of law, based on righteousness and supported by the religious conviction of the brotherhood of man, can there be any hope of a complete and satisfying life. Parchment will fail, the sword will fail, it is only the spiritual nature of man that can be triumphant.

It seems altogether probable that we can contribute most to these important objects by maintaining our position of political detachment and independence. We are not identified with any Old World interests. This position should be made more and more clear in our relations with all foreign countries. We are at peace with all of them. Our program is never to oppress, but always to assist. But while we do justice to others, we must require that justice be done to us. With us a treaty of peace means peace, and a treaty of amity means amity. We have made great contributions to the settlement of contentious differences in both Europe and Asia. But there is a very definite point beyond which we cannot go. We can only help those who help themselves. Mindful of these limitations, the one great duty that stands out requires us to use our enormous powers to trim the balance of the world.

While we can look with a great deal of pleasure upon what we have done abroad, we must remember that our continued success in that direction depends upon what we do at home. Since its very outset, it has been found necessary to conduct our government by means of political parties. That system would not have survived from generation to generation if it had not been fundamentally sound and provided the best instrumentalities for the most complete expression of the popular will. It is not necessary to claim that it has always worked perfectly. It is enough to know that nothing better has been devised. No one would deny that there should be full and free expression and an opportunity for independence of action within the party. There is no salvation in a narrow and bigoted partisanship. But if there is to be responsible party government, the party label must be something more than a mere device for securing office. Unless those who are elected under the same party designation are willing to assume sufficient responsibility and exhibit sufficient loyalty and coherence, so that they can cooperate with each other in the support of the broad general principles, of the party platform, the election is merely a mockery, no decision is made at

the polls, and there is no representation of the popular will. Common honesty and good faith with the
people who support a party at the polls require that
party, when it enters office, to assume the control of
that portion of the government to which it has been
elected. Any other course is bad faith and a violation of the party pledges.

When the country has bestowed its confidence
upon a party by making it a majority in the Congress, it has a right to expect such unity of action as
will make the party majority an effective instrument
of government. This Administration has come into
power with a very clear and definite mandate from
the people. The expression of the popular will in
favor of maintaining our constitutional guarantees
was overwhelming and decisive. There was a manifestation of such faith in the integrity of the courts
that we can consider that issue rejected for some
time to come. Likewise, the policy of public ownership of railroads and certain electric utilities met
with unmistakable defeat. The people declared that
they wanted their rights to have not a political but a
judicial determination, and their independence and
freedom continued and supported by having the
ownership and control of their property, not in the
government, but in their own hands. As they always
do when they have a fair chance, the people demonstrated that they are sound and are determined to
have a sound government.

When we turn from what was rejected to inquire what was accepted, the policy that stands out with the greatest clearness is that of economy in public expenditure with reduction and reform of taxation. The principle involved in this effort is that of conservation. The resources of this country are almost beyond computation. No mind can comprehend them. But the cost of our combined governments is likewise almost beyond definition. Not only those who are now making their tax returns, but those who meet the enhanced cost of existence in their monthly bills, know by hard experience what this great burden is and what it does. No matter what others may want, these people want a drastic economy. They are opposed to waste. They know that extravagance lengthens the hours and diminishes the rewards of their labor. I favor the policy of economy, not because I wish to save money, but because I wish to save people. The men and women of this country who toil are the ones who bear the cost of the government. Every dollar that we carelessly waste means that their life will be so much the more meager. Every dollar that we prudently save means that their life will be so much the more abundant. Economy is idealism in its most practical form.

If extravagance were not reflected in taxation, and through taxation both directly and indirectly injuriously affecting the people, it would not be of so much consequence. The wisest and soundest

Charles Lindbergh and the single-engine plane, Spirit of St. Louis, in which he made the first transatlantic solo flight in May 1927.

method of solving our tax problem is through economy. Fortunately, of all the great nations this country is best in a position to adopt that simple remedy. We do not any longer need wartime revenues. The collection of any taxes which are not absolutely required, which do not beyond reasonable doubt contribute to the public welfare, is only a species of legalized larceny. Under this republic the rewards of industry belong to those who earn them. The only constitutional tax is the tax which ministers to public necessity. The property of the country belongs to the people of the country. Their title is absolute. They do not support any privileged class; they do not need to maintain great military forces; they ought not to be burdened with a great array of public employees. They are not required to make any contribution to government expenditures except that which they voluntarily assess upon themselves through the action of their own representatives. Whenever taxes become burdensome a remedy can be applied by the people; but if they do not act for themselves, no one can be very successful in acting for them.

The time is arriving when we can have further tax reduction, when, unless we wish to hamper the people in their right to earn a living, we must have tax reform. The method of raising revenue ought not to impede the transaction of business; it ought to encourage it. I am opposed to extremely high rates, because they produce little or no revenue, because they are bad for the country, and, finally, because they are wrong. We can not finance the country, we can not improve social conditions, through any system of injustice, even if we attempt to inflict it upon the rich. Those who suffer the most harm will be the poor. This country believes in prosperity. It is absurd to suppose that it is envious of those who are already prosperous. The wise and correct course to follow in taxation and all other economic legislation is not to destroy those who have already secured success but to create conditions under which every one will have a better chance to be successful. The verdict of the country has been given on this question. That verdict stands. We shall do well to heed it.

These questions involve moral issues. We need not concern ourselves much about the rights of property if we will faithfully observe the rights of persons. Under our institutions their rights are supreme. It is not property but the right to hold property, both great and small, which our Constitution guarantees. All owners of property are charged with a service. These rights and duties have been revealed, through the conscience of society, to have a divine sanction. The very stability of our society rests upon production and conservation. For individuals or for governments to waste and squander their resources is to deny these rights and disregard these obligations. The result of economic dissipation to a nation is always moral decay.

These policies of better international understandings, greater economy, and lower taxes have contributed largely to peaceful and prosperous industrial relations. Under the helpful influences of restrictive immigration and a protective tariff, employment is plentiful, the rate of pay is high, and wage earners are in a state of contentment seldom before seen. Our transportation systems have been gradually recovering and have been able to meet all the requirements of the service. Agriculture has been very slow in reviving, but the price of cereals at last indicates that the day of its deliverance is at hand.

We are not without our problems, but our most important problem is not to secure new advantages but to maintain those which we already possess. Our system of government made up of three separate and independent departments, our divided sovereignty composed of nation and state, the matchless wisdom that is enshrined in our Constitution, all these need constant effort and tireless vigilance for their protection and support.

In a republic the first rule for the guidance of the citizen is obedience to law. Under a despotism the law may be imposed upon the subject. He has no voice in its making, no influence in its administration, it does not represent him. Under a free government the citizen makes his own laws, chooses his own administrators, which do represent him. Those who want their rights respected under the Constitution and the law ought to set the example themselves of observing the Constitution and the law. While there may be those of high intelligence who violate the law at times, the barbarian and the defective always violate it. Those who disregard the rules of society are not exhibiting a superior intelligence, are not promoting freedom and independence, are not following the path of civilization, but are displaying the traits of ignorance, of servitude, of savagery, and treading the way that leads back to the jungle.

The essence of a republic is representative government. Our Congress represents the people and the states. In all legislative affairs it is the natural collaborator with the president. In spite of all the criticism which often falls to its lot, I do not hesitate to say that there is no more independent and effective legislative body in the world. It is, and should be, jealous of its prerogative. I welcome its cooperation, and expect to share with it not only the responsibility, but the credit, for our common effort to secure beneficial legislation.

These are some of the principles which America represents. We have not by any means put them fully into practice, but we have strongly signified our belief in them. The encouraging feature of our country is not that it has reached its destination, but that it has overwhelmingly expressed its determination to proceed in the right direction. It is true that we could, with profit, be less sectional and more national in our thought. It would be well if we could replace much that is only a false and ignorant prejudice with a true and enlightened pride of race. But the last election showed that appeals to class and nationality had little effect. We were all found loyal to a common citizenship. The fundamental precept of liberty is toleration. We can not permit any inquisition either within or without the law or apply any religious test to the holding of office. The mind of America must be forever free.

It is in such contemplations, my fellow countrymen, which are not exhaustive but only representative, that I find ample warrant for satisfaction and encouragement. We should not let the much that is to do obscure the much which has been done. The past and present show faith and hope and courage fully justified. Here stands our country, an example of tranquillity at home, a patron of tranquillity abroad. Here stands its government, aware of its might but obedient to its conscience. Here it will continue to stand, seeking peace and prosperity, solicitous for the welfare of the wage earner, promoting enterprise, developing waterways and natural resources, attentive to the intuitive counsel of womanhood, encouraging education, desiring the advancement of religion, supporting the cause of justice and honor among the nations. America seeks no earthly empire built on blood and force. No ambition, no temptation, lures her to thought of foreign dominions. The legions which she sends forth are armed, not with the sword, but with the cross. The higher state to which she seeks the allegiance of all mankind is not of human, but of divine origin. She cherishes no purpose save to merit the favor of Almighty God.

Herbert Clark Hoover

31st President of the United States
1929–33

Herbert Clark Hoover

BORN: August 10, 1874, West Branch, Iowa
MARRIED: Lou Henry, Feb. 10, 1899; two children
DIED: October 20, 1964, New York, N.Y.
PARTY: Republican
EDUCATION: West Branch public schools; family-run prep school in Newburg, Ore.; youngest student in Stanford University's first class (1895).

CAREER:
International mining; became millionaire through independent enterprises (1909–14); led organizations distributing supplies to suffering Europeans (1915–19); Wilson's economic adviser at Versailles (1919); secretary of commerce under Harding and Coolidge (1921–28); president (1929–33); resided in Palo Alto, Calif.; active in humanitarian causes and federal government commissions.

PRESIDENTIAL CAMPAIGNS:
1928: Triumphed as a symbol of prosperity, winning some of the Solid South and anti-Catholic vote against Democrat Alfred E. Smith, governor of New York.
1932: The Great Depression ensured defeat by Democrat Franklin D. Roosevelt, another New York governor.

President Hoover throws out the ball to open the baseball season,
April 17, 1929.

INTRODUCTION

Herbert Hoover, like Taft, had never run for office before becoming president. But he was a national hero, whose magnificent job feeding and sustaining suffering people in Europe after the World War had given him fame as "savior of a continent."

As the bull market on Wall Street roared on, he seemed ideal to provide overexcited Americans with a wealthy engineer's sense of organization and calm judgment. Yet he told an interviewer that the public had an "exaggerated idea" of him. "They have a conviction that I am a sort of superman, that no problem is beyond my capacity."

His inaugural speech was an optimistic plea for retaining the status quo. Hoover was an ardent supporter of the Eighteenth Amendment of the Constitution, which prohibited the manufacture and sale of alcoholic beverages. He had called it "a great social and economic experiment, noble in motive and far-reaching in purpose." But the banning of liquor had generated an unprecedented national crime wave, and Hoover's words on that topic were those best remembered by the Nation.

The address was arranged by subject like a business report, a style also used by Dwight Eisenhower in his first inaugural. It was delivered to an audience sitting at the Capitol in pouring rain.

Herbert Clark Hoover
Inaugural Address

Monday, March 4, 1929

My Countrymen:
This occasion is not alone the administration of the most sacred oath which can be assumed by an American citizen. It is a dedication and consecration under God to the highest office in service of our people. I assume this trust in the humility of knowledge that only through the guidance of Almighty Providence can I hope to discharge its ever-increasing burdens.

It is in keeping with tradition throughout our history that I should express simply and directly the opinions which I hold concerning some of the matters of present importance.

OUR PROGRESS

If we survey the situation of our nation both at home and abroad, we find many satisfactions; we find some causes for concern. We have emerged from the losses of the Great War and the reconstruction following it with increased virility and strength. From this strength we have contributed to the recovery and progress of the world. What America has done has given renewed hope and courage to all who have faith in government by the people. In the large view, we have reached a higher degree of comfort and security than ever existed before in the history of the world. Through liberation from widespread poverty we have reached a higher degree of individual freedom than ever before. The devotion to and concern for our institutions are deep and sincere. We are steadily building a new race—a new civilization great in its own attainments. The influence and high purposes of our nation are respected among the peoples of the world. We aspire to distinction in the world, but to a distinction based upon confidence in our sense of justice as well as our accomplishments within our own borders and in our own lives. For wise guidance in this great period of recovery the nation is deeply indebted to Calvin Coolidge.

But all this majestic advance should not obscure the constant dangers from which self-government must be safeguarded. The strong man must at all times be alert to the attack of insidious disease.

THE FAILURE OF OUR SYSTEM OF CRIMINAL JUSTICE

The most malign of all these dangers today is disregard and disobedience of law. Crime is increasing. Confidence in rigid and speedy justice is decreasing. I am not prepared to believe that this indicates any decay in the moral fiber of the American people. I am not prepared to believe that it indicates an impotence of the federal government to enforce its laws.

It is only in part due to the additional burdens imposed upon our judicial system by the Eighteenth Amendment.[1] The problem is much wider than that. Many influences had increasingly complicated and weakened our law enforcement organization long before the adoption of the Eighteenth Amendment.

To reestablish the vigor and effectiveness of law enforcement we must critically consider the entire federal machinery of justice, the redistribution of its functions, the simplification of its procedure, the provision of additional special tribunals, the better selection of juries, and the more effective organization of our agencies of investigation and prosecution that justice may be sure and that it may be swift. While the authority of the federal government extends to but part of our vast system of national, state, and local justice, yet the standards which the federal government establishes have the most profound influence upon the whole structure.

We are fortunate in the ability and integrity of

---

1. The Eighteenth Amendment to the U.S. Constitution, ratified January 16, 1919 (effective January 16, 1920), prohibited the manufacture, sale, or transportation of intoxicating liquors within the United States and its territories. The Twenty-first Amendment (1933) repealed the Eighteenth Amendment.

our federal judges and attorneys. But the system which these officers are called upon to administer is in many respects ill adapted to present-day conditions. Its intricate and involved rules of procedure have become the refuge of both big and little criminals. There is a belief abroad that by invoking technicalities, subterfuge, and delay, the ends of justice may be thwarted by those who can pay the cost.

Reform, reorganization, and strengthening of our whole judicial and enforcement system, both in civil and criminal sides, have been advocated for years by statesmen, judges, and bar associations. First steps toward that end should not longer be delayed. Rigid and expeditious justice is the first safeguard of freedom, the basis of all ordered liberty, the vital force of progress. It must not come to be in our Republic that it can be defeated by the indifference of the citizen, by exploitation of the delays and entanglements of the law, or by combinations of criminals. Justice must not fail because the agencies of enforcement are either delinquent or inefficiently organized. To consider these evils, to find their remedy, is the most sore necessity of our times.

ENFORCEMENT OF THE EIGHTEENTH AMENDMENT

Of the undoubted abuses which have grown up under the Eighteenth Amendment, part are due to the causes I have just mentioned; but part are due

Detroit police raid an illegal underground distillery during Prohibition, 1928.

to the failure of some states to accept their share of responsibility for concurrent enforcement and to the failure of many state and local officials to accept the obligation under their oath of office zealously to enforce the laws. With the failures from these many causes has come a dangerous expansion in the criminal elements who have found enlarged opportunities in dealing in illegal liquor.

But a large responsibility rests directly upon our citizens. There would be little traffic in illegal liquor if only criminals patronized it. We must awake to the fact that this patronage from large numbers of law-abiding citizens is supplying the rewards and stimulating crime.

I have been selected by you to execute and enforce the laws of the country. I propose to do so to the extent of my own abilities, but the measure of success that the government shall attain will depend upon the moral support which you, as citizens, extend. The duty of citizens to support the laws of the land is coequal with the duty of their government to enforce the laws which exist. No greater national service can be given by men and women of good will—who, I know, are not unmindful of the responsibilities of citizenship—than that they should, by their example, assist in stamping out crime and outlawry by refusing participation in and condemning all transactions with illegal liquor. Our whole system of self-government will crumble either if officials elect what laws they will enforce or citizens elect what laws they will support. The worst evil of disregard for some law is that it destroys respect for all law. For our citizens to patronize the violation of a particular law on the ground that they are opposed to it is destructive of the very basis of all that protection of life, of homes and property which they rightly claim under other laws. If citizens do not like a law, their duty as honest men and women is to discourage its violation; their right is openly to work for its repeal.

To those of criminal mind there can be no appeal but vigorous enforcement of the law. Fortunately they are but a small percentage of our people. Their activities must be stopped.

A National Investigation

I propose to appoint a national commission for a searching investigation of the whole structure of our federal system of jurisprudence, to include the method of enforcement of the Eighteenth Amendment and the causes of abuse under it. Its purpose will be to make such recommendations for reorganization of the administration of federal laws and court procedure as may be found desirable. In the meantime it is essential that a large part of the enforcement activities be transferred from the Treasury Department to the Department of Justice as a beginning of more effective organization.

The Relation of Government to Business

The election has again confirmed the determination of the American people that regulation of private enterprise and not government ownership or operation is the course rightly to be pursued in our relation to business. In recent years we have established a differentiation in the whole method of business regulation between the industries which produce and distribute commodities on the one hand and public utilities on the other. In the former, our laws insist upon effective competition; in the latter, because we substantially confer a monopoly by limiting competition, we must regulate their services and rates. The rigid enforcement of the laws applicable to both groups is the very base of equal opportunity and freedom from domination for all our people, and it is just as essential for the stability and prosperity of business itself as for the protection of the public at large. Such regulation should be extended by the federal government within the limitations of the Constitution and only when the individual states are without power to protect their citizens through their own authority. On the other hand, we should be fearless when the authority rests only in the federal government.

COOPERATION BY THE GOVERNMENT

The larger purpose of our economic thought should be to establish more firmly stability and security of business and employment and thereby remove poverty still further from our borders. Our people have in recent years developed a new-found capacity for cooperation among themselves to effect high purposes in public welfare. It is an advance toward the highest conception of self-government. Self-government does not and should not imply the use of political agencies alone. Progress is born of cooperation in the community—not from governmental restraints. The government should assist and encourage these movements of collective self-help by itself cooperating with them. Business has by cooperation made great progress in the advancement of service, in stability, in regularity of employment and in the correction of its own abuses. Such progress, however, can continue only so long as business manifests its respect for law.

There is an equally important field of cooperation by the federal government with the multitude of agencies, state, municipal and private, in the systematic development of those processes which directly affect public health, recreation, education, and the home. We have need further to perfect the means by which government can be adapted to human service.

Families made homeless by the Great Depression built shacktowns called Hoovervilles. Seattle, Washington, July 20, 1932.

EDUCATION

Although education is primarily a responsibility of the states and local communities, and rightly so, yet the nation as a whole is vitally concerned in its development everywhere to the highest standards and to complete universality. Self-government can succeed only through an instructed electorate. Our objective is not simply to overcome illiteracy. The nation has marched far beyond that. The more complex the problems of the nation become, the greater is the need for more and more advanced instruction. Moreover, as our numbers increase and as our life expands with science and invention, we must discover more and more leaders for every walk of life. We can not hope to succeed in directing this increasingly complex civilization unless we can draw all the talent of leadership from the whole people. One civilization after another has been wrecked upon the attempt to secure sufficient leadership from a single group or class. If we would prevent the growth of class distinctions and would constantly refresh our leadership with the ideals of our people, we must draw constantly from the general mass. The full opportunity for every boy and girl to rise through the selective processes of education can alone secure to us this leadership.

Public Health

In public health the discoveries of science have opened a new era. Many sections of our country and many groups of our citizens suffer from diseases the eradication of which are mere matters of administration and moderate expenditure. Public health service should be as fully organized and as universally incorporated into our governmental system as is public education. The returns are a thousand fold in economic benefits, and infinitely more in reduction of suffering and promotion of human happiness.

World Peace

The United States fully accepts the profound truth that our own progress, prosperity, and peace are interlocked with the progress, prosperity, and peace of all humanity. The whole world is at peace. The dangers to a continuation of this peace today are largely the fear and suspicion which still haunt the world. No suspicion or fear can be rightly directed toward our country.

Those who have a true understanding of America know that we have no desire for territorial expansion, for economic or other domination of other peoples. Such purposes are repugnant to our ideals of human freedom. Our form of government is ill adapted to the responsibilities which inevitably follow permanent limitation of the independence of other peoples. Superficial observers seem to find no destiny for our abounding increase in population, in wealth and power except that of imperialism. They fail to see that the American people are engrossed in the building for themselves of a new economic system, a new social system, a new political system all of which are characterized by aspirations of freedom of opportunity and thereby are the negation of imperialism. They fail to realize that because of our abounding prosperity our youth are pressing more and more into our institutions of learning; that our people are seeking a larger vision through art, literature, science, and travel; that they are moving toward stronger moral and spiritual life—that from these things our sympathies are broadening beyond the bounds of our nation and race toward their true expression in a real brotherhood of man. They fail to see that the idealism of America will lead it to no narrow or selfish channel, but inspire it to do its full share as a nation toward the advancement of civilization. It will do that not by mere declaration but by taking a practical part in supporting all useful international undertakings. We not only desire peace with the world, but to see peace maintained throughout the world. We wish to advance the reign of justice and reason toward the extinction of force.

The recent treaty[2] for the renunciation of war as an instrument of national policy sets an advanced standard in our conception of the relations of nations. Its acceptance should pave the way to greater limitation of armament, the offer of which we sincerely extend to the world. But its full realization also implies a greater and greater perfection in the instrumentalities for pacific settlement of controversies between nations. In the creation and use of these instrumentalities we should support every sound method of conciliation, arbitration, and judicial settlement. American statesmen were among the first to propose and they have constantly urged upon the world, the establishment of a tribunal for the settlement of controversies of a justiciable character. The Permanent Court of International Justice in its major purpose is thus peculiarly identified with American ideals and with American statesmanship. No more potent instrumentality for this purpose has ever been conceived and no other is practicable of establishment. The reservations placed upon our adherence should not be misinterpreted. The United States seeks by these reservations no special privilege or advantage but only to clarify our relation to advisory opinions and

---

2. Kellogg-Briand Pact of 1928, ultimately ratified by sixty-two countries, including the United States, provided for "a renunciation of war as an instrument of national policy."

other matters which are subsidiary to the major purpose of the court. The way should, and I believe will, be found by which we may take our proper place in a movement so fundamental to the progress of peace.

Our people have determined that we should make no political engagements such as membership in the League of Nations,[3] which may commit us in advance as a nation to become involved in the settlements of controversies between other countries. They adhere to the belief that the independence of America from such obligations increases its ability and availability for service in all fields of human progress.

I have lately returned from a journey among our sister republics of the Western Hemisphere. I have received unbounded hospitality and courtesy as their expression of friendliness to our country. We are held by particular bonds of sympathy and common interest with them. They are each of them building a racial character and a culture which is an impressive contribution to human progress. We wish only for the maintenance of their independ-

---

3. League of Nations (1920–46) was created by the victorious powers in the First World War through the Treaty of Versailles. The aims of this international organization were to promote international cooperation and to achieve international peace and security. Although President Woodrow Wilson received the Nobel Peace Prize for his role in creating the League of Nations, the U.S. Senate never ratified the Treaty of Versailles, and, thus, the United States never joined.

ence, the growth of their stability, and their prosperity. While we have had wars in the Western Hemisphere, yet on the whole the record is in encouraging contrast with that of other parts of the world. Fortunately the New World is largely free from the inheritances of fear and distrust which have so troubled the Old World. We should keep it so.

It is impossible, my countrymen, to speak of peace without profound emotion. In thousands of homes in America, in millions of homes around the world, there are vacant chairs. It would be a shameful confession of our unworthiness if it should develop that we have abandoned the hope for which all these men died. Surely civilization is old enough, surely mankind is mature enough so that we ought in our own lifetime to find a way to permanent peace. Abroad, to west and east, are nations whose sons mingled their blood with the blood of our sons on the battlefields. Most of these nations have contributed to our race, to our culture, our knowledge, and our progress. From one of them we derive our very language and from many of them much of the genius of our institutions. Their desire for peace is as deep and sincere as our own.

Peace can be contributed to by respect for our ability in defense. Peace can be promoted by the limitation of arms and by the creation of the instrumentalities for peaceful settlement of controversies. But it will become a reality only through self-restraint and active effort in friendliness and helpfulness. I covet for this administration a record of having further contributed to advance the cause of peace.

PARTY RESPONSIBILITIES

In our form of democracy the expression of the popular will can be effected only through the instrumentality of political parties. We maintain party government not to promote intolerant partisanship but because opportunity must be given for expression of the popular will, and organization provided for the execution of its mandates and for accountability of government to the people. It follows that the government both in the executive and the legislative branches must carry out in good faith the platforms upon which the party was entrusted with power. But the government is that of the whole people; the party is the instrument through which policies are determined and men chosen to bring them into being. The animosities of elections should have no place in our government, for government must concern itself alone with the common weal.

SPECIAL SESSION OF THE CONGRESS

Action upon some of the proposals upon which the Republican Party was returned to power, particularly further agricultural relief and limited changes in the tariff, cannot in justice to our farmers, our labor, and our manufacturers be postponed. I shall therefore request a special session of Congress for the consideration of these two questions. I shall deal with each of them upon the assembly of the Congress.

OTHER MANDATES FROM THE ELECTION

It appears to me that the more important further mandates from the recent election were the maintenance of the integrity of the Constitution; the vigorous enforcement of the laws; the continuance of economy in public expenditure; the continued regulation of business to prevent domination in the community; the denial of ownership or operation of business by the government in competition with its citizens; the avoidance of policies which would involve us in the controversies of foreign nations; the more effective reorganization of the departments of the federal government; the expansion of public works; and the promotion of welfare activities affecting education and the home.

These were the more tangible determinations of the election, but beyond them was the confidence and belief of the people that we would not neglect the support of the embedded ideals and aspirations of America. These ideals and aspirations are the touchstones upon which the day-to-day administration and legislative acts of government must be tested. More than this, the Government must, so far as lies within its proper powers, give leadership to the realization of these ideals and to the fruition of these aspirations. No one can adequately reduce these things of the spirit to phrases or to a catalogue of definitions. We do know what the attainments of these ideals should be: The preservation of self-government and its full foundations in local government; the perfection of justice whether in economic or in social fields; the maintenance of ordered liberty; the denial of domination by any group or class; the building up and preservation of equality of opportunity; the stimulation of initiative and individuality; absolute integrity in public affairs; the choice of officials for fitness to office; the direction of economic progress toward prosperity for the further lessening of poverty; the freedom of public opinion; the sustaining of education and of the advancement of knowledge; the growth of religious spirit and the tolerance of all faiths; the strengthening of the home; the advancement of peace.

There is no short road to the realization of these aspirations. Ours is a progressive people, but with a determination that progress must be based upon the foundation of experience. Ill-considered remedies for our faults bring only penalties after them. But if we hold the faith of the men in our mighty past who created these ideals, we shall leave them heightened and strengthened for our children.

CONCLUSION

This is not the time and place for extended discussion. The questions before our country are problems of progress to higher standards; they are not the problems of degeneration. They demand thought and they serve to quicken the conscience and enlist our sense of responsibility for their settlement. And that responsibility rests upon you, my countrymen, as much as upon those of us who have been selected for office.

Ours is a land rich in resources; stimulating in its glorious beauty; filled with millions of happy homes; blessed with comfort and opportunity. In no nation are the institutions of progress more advanced. In no nation are the fruits of accomplishment more secure. In no nation is the government more worthy of respect. No country is more loved by its people. I have an abiding faith in their capacity, integrity and high purpose. I have no fears for the future of our country. It is bright with hope.

In the presence of my countrymen, mindful of the solemnity of this occasion, knowing what the task means and the responsibility which it involves, I beg your tolerance, your aid, and your cooperation. I ask the help of Almighty God in this service to my country to which you have called me.

Franklin Delano Roosevelt

32nd President of the United States
1933–45

Franklin Delano Roosevelt

BORN: January 30, 1882, Hyde Park, N.Y.
MARRIED: Anna Eleanor Roosevelt, March 17, 1905;
six children
DIED: April 12, 1945, Warm Springs, Ga.
PARTY: Democratic
EDUCATION: Privately tutored; Groton (1896–1900);
Harvard College (1903); Columbia University Law
School (1904–07); left upon passing the bar.

CAREER:
Private law firm; New York State Senate (1911–13); assistant secretary of the navy (1913–20); unsuccessful candidate for vice president (1920); governor of New York
(1929–1933); president (1933–45); died in office.

PRESIDENTIAL CAMPAIGNS:
1932: Incumbent Hoover soundly beaten by Roosevelt
and Congressman John Nance Garner of Texas.
1936: In most crushing victory since 1820, defeated
Kansas Governor Alfred M. Landon.
1940: In unprecedented third campaign, Roosevelt and
Henry Wallace defeated Hoosier Wendell L. Willkie.
1944: Roosevelt, now running with Truman, defeated
Republican New York Governor Thomas E. Dewey,
becoming the only four-term president. That led to the
Twenty-second Amendment, which sets a two-term limit.

Photographic montage of President Franklin D. Roosevelt's first inaugural address (March 4, 1933); banner shows its most memorable line.

INTRODUCTION

Franklin Roosevelt, bearer of a proud name, sought to follow his cousin Theodore, whose manner he copied in many ways. His marriage to Teddy Roosevelt's niece brought him closer to his hero.

After the collapse of the stock market in 1929 and the onset of the Great Depression, it was impossible to imagine that the next president would not be a Democrat. The governor of New York was a natural choice. Yet, a prominent journalist said Roosevelt "is a pleasant man who, without any important qualifications for the office, would very much like to be president."

Roosevelt was so badly affected by polio that he could not walk unaided. Thus, he was an appropriate symbol of a country that also was paralyzed—economically and emotionally. Like him, the people were eager to get moving again. Roosevelt showed his energy by flying to Chicago to become the first candidate to address the nominating convention that chose him as their standard-bearer.

The eloquence he displayed in his inaugural was the most candid and also the most reassuring that had ever been given in a crisis by a president. Roosevelt manifested his role as a leader not only by his strong words but also by his forceful warning that if Congress did not respond to his calls for action, he would, without hesitation, proceed on his own.

Franklin Delano Roosevelt
First Inaugural Address

Saturday, March 4, 1933

I am certain that my fellow Americans expect that on my induction into the presidency I will address them with a candor and a decision which the present situation of our nation impels. This is preeminently the time to speak the truth, the whole truth, frankly and boldly. Nor need we shrink from honestly facing conditions in our country today. This great nation will endure as it has endured, will revive and will prosper. So, first of all, let me assert my firm belief that the only thing we have to fear is fear itself—nameless, unreasoning, unjustified terror which paralyzes needed efforts to convert retreat into advance. In every dark hour of our national life a leadership of frankness and vigor has met with that understanding and support of the people themselves which is essential to victory. I am convinced that you will again give that support to leadership in these critical days.

In such a spirit on my part and on yours we face our common difficulties. They concern, thank God, only material things. Values have shrunken to fantastic levels; taxes have risen; our ability to pay has fallen; government of all kinds is faced by serious curtailment of income; the means of exchange are frozen in the currents of trade; the withered leaves of industrial enterprise lie on every side; farmers find no markets for their produce; the savings of many years in thousands of families are gone.

More important, a host of unemployed citizens face the grim problem of existence, and an equally great number toil with little return. Only a foolish optimist can deny the dark realities of the moment.

Yet our distress comes from no failure of substance. We are stricken by no plague of locusts. Compared with the perils which our forefathers conquered because they believed and were not afraid, we have still much to be thankful for. Nature still offers her bounty and human efforts have multiplied it. Plenty is at our doorstep, but a generous use of it languishes in the very sight of the supply. Primarily this is because the rulers of the exchange of mankind's goods have failed, through their own stubbornness and their own incompetence, have admitted their failure, and abdicated. Practices of the unscrupulous money changers stand indicted in the court of public opinion, rejected by the hearts and minds of men.

True they have tried, but their efforts have been cast in the pattern of an outworn tradition. Faced by failure of credit they have proposed only the lending of more money. Stripped of the lure of profit by which to induce our people to follow their false leadership, they have resorted to exhortations,

Hungry men wait in a breadline to be fed in New York City, 1932.

pleading tearfully for restored confidence. They know only the rules of a generation of self-seekers. They have no vision, and when there is no vision the people perish.

The money changers have fled from their high seats in the temple of our civilization. We may now restore that temple to the ancient truths. The measure of the restoration lies in the extent to which we apply social values more noble than mere monetary profit.

Happiness lies not in the mere possession of money; it lies in the joy of achievement, in the thrill of creative effort. The joy and moral stimulation of work no longer must be forgotten in the mad chase of evanescent profits. These dark days will be worth all they cost us if they teach us that our true destiny is not to be ministered unto but to minister to ourselves and to our fellow men.

Recognition of the falsity of material wealth as the standard of success goes hand in hand with the abandonment of the false belief that public office and high political position are to be valued only by the standards of pride of place and personal profit; and there must be an end to a conduct in banking and in business which too often has given to a sacred trust the likeness of callous and selfish wrongdoing. Small wonder that confidence languishes, for it thrives only on honesty, on honor, on the sacredness of obligations, on faithful protection, on unselfish performance; without them it cannot live.

Restoration calls, however, not for changes in ethics alone. This nation asks for action, and action now.

Our greatest primary task is to put people to work. This is no unsolvable problem if we face it wisely and courageously. It can be accomplished in part by direct recruiting by the government itself, treating the task as we would treat the emergency of a war, but at the same time, through this employment, accomplishing greatly needed projects to stimulate and reorganize the use of our natural resources.

Hand in hand with this we must frankly recognize the overbalance of population in our industrial centers and, by engaging on a national scale in a redistribution, endeavor to provide a better use of the land for those best fitted for the land. The task can be helped by definite efforts to raise the values of agricultural products and with this the power to purchase the output of our cities. It can be helped by preventing realistically the tragedy of the growing loss through foreclosure of our small homes and our farms. It can be helped by insistence that the federal, state, and local governments act forthwith on the demand that their cost be drastically reduced. It can be helped by the unifying of relief activities which today are often scattered, uneconomical, and unequal. It can be helped by national planning for and supervision of all forms of transportation and of communications and other utili-

A migrant mother of seven who found work as a pea picker in California during the Great Depression. Photo by Dorothea Lange for the Farm Security Administration, February 1936.

ties which have a definitely public character. There are many ways in which it can be helped, but it can never be helped merely by talking about it. We must act and act quickly.

Finally, in our progress toward a resumption of work we require two safeguards against a return of the evils of the old order; there must be a strict supervision of all banking and credits and investments; there must be an end to speculation with other people's money, and there must be provision for an adequate but sound currency.

There are the lines of attack. I shall presently urge upon a new Congress in special session detailed measures for their fulfillment, and I shall seek the immediate assistance of the several States.

Through this program of action we address ourselves to putting our own national house in order and making income balance outgo. Our international trade relations, though vastly important, are in point of time and necessity secondary to the establishment of a sound national economy. I favor as a practical policy the putting of first things first. I shall spare no effort to restore world trade by international economic readjustment, but the emergency at home cannot wait on that accomplishment.

The basic thought that guides these specific means of national recovery is not narrowly nationalistic. It is the insistence, as a first consideration, upon the interdependence of the various elements in all parts of the United States—a recognition of the old and permanently important manifestation of the American spirit of the pioneer. It is the way to recovery. It is the immediate way. It is the strongest assurance that the recovery will endure.

In the field of world policy I would dedicate this nation to the policy of the good neighbor—the neighbor who resolutely respects himself and, because he does so, respects the rights of others— the neighbor who respects his obligations and respects the sanctity of his agreements in and with a world of neighbors.

If I read the temper of our people correctly, we now realize as we have never realized before our interdependence on each other; that we can not merely take but we must give as well; that if we are to go forward, we must move as a trained and loyal army willing to sacrifice for the good of a common discipline, because without such discipline no progress is made, no leadership becomes effective. We are, I know, ready and willing to submit our lives and property to such discipline, because it makes possible a leadership which aims at a larger good. This I propose to offer, pledging that the larger purposes will bind upon us all as a sacred obligation with a unity of duty hitherto evoked only in time of armed strife.

With this pledge taken, I assume unhesitatingly the leadership of this great army of our people dedicated to a disciplined attack upon our common problems.

Action in this image and to this end is feasible under the form of government which we have inherited from our ancestors. Our Constitution is so simple and practical that it is possible always to meet extraordinary needs by changes in emphasis and arrangement without loss of essential form. That is why our constitutional system has proved itself the most superbly enduring political mechanism the modern world has produced. It has met every stress of vast expansion of territory, of foreign wars, of bitter internal strife, of world relations.

It is to be hoped that the normal balance of executive and legislative authority may be wholly adequate to meet the unprecedented task before us. But it may be that an unprecedented demand and need for undelayed action may call for temporary departure from that normal balance of public procedure.

I am prepared under my constitutional duty to recommend the measures that a stricken nation in the midst of a stricken world may require. These measures, or such other measures as the Congress may build out of its experience and wisdom, I shall seek, within my constitutional authority, to bring to speedy adoption.

But in the event that the Congress shall fail to take one of these two courses, and in the event that the national emergency is still critical, I shall not

Dust storms caused by drought and erosion ravage the Great Plains and add to the hardship of the economic depression, Rolla, Kansas, May 6, 1935.

evade the clear course of duty that will then confront me. I shall ask the Congress for the one remaining instrument to meet the crisis—broad Executive power to wage a war against the emergency, as great as the power that would be given to me if we were in fact invaded by a foreign foe.

For the trust reposed in me I will return the courage and the devotion that befit the time. I can do no less.

We face the arduous days that lie before us in the warm courage of the national unity; with the clear consciousness of seeking old and precious moral values; with the clean satisfaction that comes from the stern performance of duty by old and young alike. We aim at the assurance of a rounded and permanent national life.

We do not distrust the future of essential democracy. The people of the United States have not failed. In their need they have registered a mandate that they want direct, vigorous action. They have asked for discipline and direction under leadership. They have made me the present instrument of their wishes. In the spirit of the gift I take it.

In this dedication of a nation we humbly ask the blessing of God. May He protect each and every one of us. May He guide me in the days to come.

The vast legislative programs constituting the substance of the New Deal in America gave Roosevelt much to talk about and to elaborate on. Their popularity had been demonstrated by his reelection, when he carried forty-six of the then–forty-eight states.

This inauguration was the first to be held on January 20—in conformity with the change provided in the Twentieth Amendment to the Constitution to get the president sworn into office sooner than March 4. Historically, January 20 had a record of good weather in Washington, but on this occasion 1.77 inches of almost-freezing rain fell, soaking the president and the First Lady to the skin as they rode in an open limousine and later watched the inaugural parade. Twice during his delivery of the address, the president tried to wipe his face dry.

Roosevelt's words were partially the work of Samuel Rosenman, a former New York judge, who worked as a close assistant to the president. They constitute a major salute to the principle that it is legitimate for government to act on behalf of the needs of the people—in short, a significant argument for what is known today as big government. National needs were great, the president declared earnestly. A particular sentence became famous: "I see one-third of a nation ill-housed, ill-clad, ill-nourished."

Franklin Delano Roosevelt
Second Inaugural Address

Wednesday, January 20, 1937[1]

When four years ago we met to inaugurate a president, the Republic, single-minded in anxiety, stood in spirit here. We dedicated ourselves to the fulfillment of a vision—to speed the time when there would be for all the people that security and peace essential to the pursuit of happiness. We of the Republic pledged ourselves to drive from the temple of our ancient faith those who had profaned it; to end by action, tireless and unafraid, the stagnation and despair of that day. We did those first things first.

Our covenant with ourselves did not stop there. Instinctively we recognized a deeper need—the need to find through government the instrument of our united purpose to solve for the individual the ever-rising problems of a complex civilization. Repeated attempts at their solution without the aid of government had left us baffled

---

1. The Twentieth Amendment to the U.S. Constitution, ratified in 1933, changed the ending dates for the term of the president and vice president from March 4 to noon on January 20. It was felt that speed of twentieth-century communications and transportation made it unnecessary to have such a long gap between election and inauguration. Other clauses dealt with terms of Congress and presidential succession.

and bewildered. For, without that aid, we had been unable to create those moral controls over the services of science which are necessary to make science a useful servant instead of a ruthless master of mankind. To do this we knew that we must find practical controls over blind economic forces and blindly selfish men.

We of the Republic sensed the truth that democratic government has innate capacity to protect its people against disasters once considered inevitable, to solve problems once considered unsolvable. We would not admit that we could not find a way to master economic epidemics just as, after centuries of fatalistic suffering, we had found a way to master epidemics of disease. We refused to leave the problems of our common welfare to be solved by the winds of chance and the hurricanes of disaster.

In this we Americans were discovering no wholly new truth; we were writing a new chapter in our book of self-government.

This year marks the one hundred and fiftieth anniversary of the Constitutional Convention which made us a nation. At that Convention our forefathers found the way out of the chaos which followed the Revolutionary War; they created a strong government with powers of united action sufficient then and now to solve problems utterly beyond individual or local solution. A century and a half ago they established the federal government

President Franklin Roosevelt addresses the American people by radio in one of his frequent fireside chats, Washington, D.C., April 28, 1935.

in order to promote the general welfare and secure the blessings of liberty to the American people.

Today we invoke those same powers of government to achieve the same objectives.

Four years of new experience have not belied our historic instinct. They hold out the clear hope that government within communities, government within the separate states, and government of the United States can do the things the times require, without yielding its democracy. Our tasks in the last four years did not force democracy to take a holiday.

Nearly all of us recognize that as intricacies of human relationships increase, so power to govern them also must increase—power to stop evil; power to do good. The essential democracy of our Nation and the safety of our people depend not upon the absence of power, but upon lodging it with those whom the people can change or continue at stated intervals through an honest and free system of elections. The Constitution of 1787 did not make our democracy impotent.

In fact, in these last four years, we have made the exercise of all power more democratic; for we have begun to bring private autocratic powers into their proper subordination to the public's government. The legend that they were invincible—above and beyond the processes of a democracy—has been shattered. They have been challenged and beaten.

Our progress out of the depression is obvious. But that is not all that you and I mean by the new order of things. Our pledge was not merely to do a patchwork job with secondhand materials. By using the new materials of social justice we have undertaken to erect on the old foundations a more enduring structure for the better use of future generations.

In that purpose we have been helped by achievements of mind and spirit. Old truths have been relearned; untruths have been unlearned. We have always known that heedless self-interest was bad morals; we know now that it is bad economics. Out of the collapse of a prosperity whose builders boasted their practicality has come the conviction that in the long run economic morality pays. We are beginning to wipe out the line that divides the practical from the ideal; and in so doing we are fashioning an instrument of unimagined power for the establishment of a morally better world.

This new understanding undermines the old admiration of worldly success as such. We are beginning to abandon our tolerance of the abuse of power by those who betray for profit the elementary decencies of life.

In this process evil things formerly accepted will not be so easily condoned. Hardheadedness will not so easily excuse hardheartedness. We are moving toward an era of good feeling. But we realize that there can be no era of good feeling save among men of good will.

For these reasons I am justified in believing that the greatest change we have witnessed has been the change in the moral climate of America.

Among men of good will, science and democracy together offer an ever-richer life and ever-larger satisfaction to the individual. With this change in our moral climate and our rediscovered ability to improve our economic order, we have set our feet upon the road of enduring progress.

Shall we pause now and turn our back upon the road that lies ahead? Shall we call this the promised land? Or, shall we continue on our way? For "each age is a dream that is dying, or one that is coming to birth."[2]

Many voices are heard as we face a great decision. Comfort says, "Tarry a while." Opportunism says, "This is a good spot." Timidity asks, "How difficult is the road ahead?"

True, we have come far from the days of stagnation and despair. Vitality has been preserved. Courage and confidence have been restored. Mental and moral horizons have been extended.

But our present gains were won under the pressure of more than ordinary circumstances. Advance

---

2. Ode: "We are the music-makers," by English poet Arthur O'Shaughnessy (1844–81).

became imperative under the goad of fear and suffering. The times were on the side of progress.

To hold to progress today, however, is more difficult. Dulled conscience, irresponsibility, and ruthless self-interest already reappear. Such symptoms of prosperity may become portents of disaster! Prosperity already tests the persistence of our progressive purpose.

Let us ask again: Have we reached the goal of our vision of that fourth day of March 1933? Have we found our happy valley?

I see a great nation, upon a great continent, blessed with a great wealth of natural resources. Its hundred and thirty million people are at peace among themselves; they are making their country a good neighbor among the nations. I see a United States which can demonstrate that, under democratic methods of government, national wealth can be translated into a spreading volume of human comforts hitherto unknown, and the lowest standard of living can be raised far above the level of mere subsistence.

But here is the challenge to our democracy: In this nation I see tens of millions of its citizens—a substantial part of its whole population—who at this very moment are denied the greater part of what the very lowest standards of today call the necessities of life.

I see millions of families trying to live on

Drought causes families like the Evanses of South Dakota to migrate west. Sign on car says Oregon or bust, *1935.*

incomes so meager that the pall of family disaster hangs over them day by day.

I see millions whose daily lives in city and on farm continue under conditions labeled indecent by a so-called polite society half a century ago.

I see millions denied education, recreation, and the opportunity to better their lot and the lot of their children.

I see millions lacking the means to buy the products of farm and factory and by their poverty denying work and productiveness to many other millions.

I see one-third of a nation ill-housed, ill-clad, ill-nourished.

It is not in despair that I paint you that picture. I paint it for you in hope—because the nation, seeing and understanding the injustice in it, proposes to paint it out. We are determined to make every American citizen the subject of his country's interest and concern; and we will never regard any faithful law-abiding group within our borders as superfluous. The test of our progress is not whether we add more to the abundance of those who have much; it is whether we provide enough for those who have too little.

If I know aught of the spirit and purpose of our nation, we will not listen to Comfort, Opportunism, and Timidity. We will carry on.

Overwhelmingly, we of the Republic are men and women of good will; men and women who have more than warm hearts of dedication; men and women who have cool heads and willing hands of practical purpose as well. They will insist that every agency of popular government use effective instruments to carry out their will.

Government is competent when all who compose it work as trustees for the whole people. It can make constant progress when it keeps abreast of all the facts. It can obtain justified support and legitimate criticism when the people receive true information of all that government does.

If I know aught of the will of our people, they will demand that these conditions of effective government shall be created and maintained. They will demand a nation uncorrupted by cancers of injustice and, therefore, strong among the nations in its example of the will to peace.

Today we reconsecrate our country to long-cherished ideals in a suddenly changed civilization. In every land there are always at work forces that drive men apart and forces that draw men together. In our personal ambitions we are individualists. But in our seeking for economic and political progress as a nation, we all go up, or else we all go down, as one people.

To maintain a democracy of effort requires a vast amount of patience in dealing with differing methods, a vast amount of humility. But out of the confusion of many voices rises an understanding of dominant public need. Then political leadership can voice common ideals, and aid in their realization.

In taking again the oath of office as president of the United States, I assume the solemn obligation of leading the American people forward along the road over which they have chosen to advance.

While this duty rests upon me I shall do my utmost to speak their purpose and to do their will, seeking Divine guidance to help us each and every one to give light to them that sit in darkness and to guide our feet into the way of peace.

INTRODUCTION

War in Europe broke out in September 1939. Defenseless democracies—Norway, Luxembourg, Denmark, Belgium, and the Netherlands—quickly fell to the Nazis. By June 1940, France, too, surrendered and was occupied by Germany.

In this grim time, Roosevelt played coyly with Democratic leaders about his availability. It had been a tradition since George Washington that presidents did not seek a third term. But most Democrats were sure that only Roosevelt could win. "Draft Roosevelt" clubs arose throughout the country. At the convention, the chairman, Kentucky Senator Alben W. Barkley, revealed a message from Roosevelt that the delegates were free to choose any candidate they wished. Concluding that Roosevelt himself might be among them, they nominated him on the first roll call.

As the Nazi air assault on Britain grew more intense in the summer of 1940, support for Roosevelt also grew stronger, the public seeing him as most able to stand up to Hitler. Still, Roosevelt declared during the campaign, "I have said this before, but I shall say it again and again and again: Your boys are not going to be sent into foreign wars."

Roosevelt rewrote this address seven times. More abstract and philosophical than his previous two, it displays the help he had from his friends, poet Archibald MacLeish and playwright Robert E. Sherwood.

152

Franklin Delano Roosevelt
Third Inaugural Address

Monday, January 20, 1941

On each national day of inauguration since 1789, the people have renewed their sense of dedication to the United States.

In Washington's day the task of the people was to create and weld together a nation.

In Lincoln's day the task of the people was to preserve that nation from disruption from within.

In this day the task of the people is to save that Nation and its institutions from disruption from without.

To us there has come a time, in the midst of swift happenings, to pause for a moment and take stock—to recall what our place in history has been, and to rediscover what we are and what we may be. If we do not, we risk the real peril of inaction.

Lives of nations are determined not by the count of years, but by the lifetime of the human spirit. The life of a man is three-score years and ten: a little more, a little less. The life of a nation is the fullness of the measure of its will to live.

There are men who doubt this. There are men who believe that democracy, as a form of government and a frame of life, is limited or measured by a kind of mystical and artificial fate that, for some unexplained reason, tyranny and slavery have become the surging wave of the future—and that freedom is an ebbing tide.

But we Americans know that this is not true.

Eight years ago, when the life of this republic seemed frozen by a fatalistic terror, we proved that this is not true. We were in the midst of shock—but we acted. We acted quickly, boldly, decisively.

These later years have been living years—fruitful years for the people of this democracy. For they have brought to us greater security and, I hope, a better understanding that life's ideals are to be measured in other than material things.

Most vital to our present and our future is this experience of a democracy which successfully survived crisis at home; put away many evil things; built new structures on enduring lines; and, through it all, maintained the fact of its democracy.

For action has been taken within the three-way framework of the Constitution of the United States. The coordinate branches of the government continue freely to function. The Bill of Rights remains inviolate. The freedom of elections is wholly maintained. Prophets of the downfall of American democracy have seen their dire predictions come to naught.

Democracy is not dying.

We know it because we have seen it revive—and grow.

We know it cannot die—because it is built on

President Franklin and Eleanor Roosevelt ride in an open car on inauguration day, January 20, 1941.

Massive public works projects like the Tennessee Valley Authority's Douglas Dam on the French Broad River put people back to work, June 1942.

the unhampered initiative of individual men and women joined together in a common enterprise—an enterprise undertaken and carried through by the free expression of a free majority.

We know it because democracy alone, of all forms of government, enlists the full force of men's enlightened will.

We know it because democracy alone has constructed an unlimited civilization capable of infinite progress in the improvement of human life.

We know it because, if we look below the surface, we sense it still spreading on every continent—for it is the most humane, the most advanced, and in the end the most unconquerable of all forms of human society.

A nation, like a person, has a body—a body that must be fed and clothed and housed, invigorated and rested, in a manner that measures up to the objectives of our time.

A nation, like a person, has a mind—a mind that must be kept informed and alert, that must know itself, that understands the hopes and the needs of its neighbors—all the other nations that live within the narrowing circle of the world.

And a nation, like a person, has something deeper, something more permanent, something larger than the sum of all its parts. It is that something which matters most to its future—which calls forth the most sacred guarding of its present.

After the Japanese raid on Pearl Harbor, Hawaii, December 7, 1941.

It is a thing for which we find it difficult—even impossible—to hit upon a single, simple word.

And yet we all understand what it is—the spirit—the faith of America. It is the product of centuries. It was born in the multitudes of those who came from many lands—some of high degree, but mostly plain people, who sought here, early and late, to find freedom more freely.

The democratic aspiration is no mere recent phase in human history. It is human history. It permeated the ancient life of early peoples. It blazed anew in the middle ages. It was written in Magna Carta.[1]

In the Americas its impact has been irresistible. America has been the New World in all tongues, to all peoples, not because this continent was a new-found land, but because all those who came here believed they could create upon this continent a new life—a life that should be new in freedom.

Its vitality was written into our own Mayflower Compact,[2] into the Declaration of Independence, into the Constitution of the United States, into the Gettysburg Address.

---

1. The Magna Carta (1215) contains a series of concessions wrung from the unwilling King John of England by his rebellious barons. By establishing for the first time that the power of a government could be constrained by written agreement with the governed, it is considered a cornerstone of liberty in Anglo–Saxon constitutional law.
2. The Mayflower Compact (1620) was drawn up by the Pilgrims before disembarking from their ship at Plymouth Colony, Massachusetts. It established the first basis for written laws in the New World.

Those who first came here to carry out the longings of their spirit, and the millions who followed, and the stock that sprang from them—all have moved forward constantly and consistently toward an ideal which in itself has gained stature and clarity with each generation.

The hopes of the Republic cannot forever tolerate either undeserved poverty or self-serving wealth.

We know that we still have far to go; that we must more greatly build the security and the opportunity and the knowledge of every citizen, in the measure justified by the resources and the capacity of the land.

But it is not enough to achieve these purposes alone. It is not enough to clothe and feed the body of this nation, and instruct and inform its mind. For there is also the spirit. And of the three, the greatest is the spirit.

Without the body and the mind, as all men know, the Nation could not live.

But if the spirit of America were killed, even though the Nation's body and mind, constricted in an alien world, lived on, the America we know would have perished.

That spirit—that faith—speaks to us in our daily lives in ways often unnoticed, because they seem so obvious. It speaks to us here in the Capital of the Nation. It speaks to us through the processes of governing in the sovereignties of forty-eight states. It

A young Japanese American waits to leave with her family for a U.S. internment camp, April 1942.

speaks to us in our counties, in our cities, in our towns, and in our villages. It speaks to us from the other nations of the hemisphere, and from those across the seas—the enslaved, as well as the free. Sometimes we fail to hear or heed these voices of freedom because to us the privilege of our freedom is such an old, old story.

The destiny of America was proclaimed in words of prophecy spoken by our first president in his first inaugural in 1789—words almost directed, it would seem, to this year of 1941: "The preservation of the sacred fire of liberty and the destiny of the republican model of government are justly considered . . . deeply, . . . finally, staked on the experiment intrusted to the hands of the American people."

If we lose that sacred fire—if we let it be smothered with doubt and fear—then we shall reject the destiny which Washington strove so valiantly and so triumphantly to establish. The preservation of the spirit and faith of the nation does, and will, furnish the highest justification for every sacrifice that we may make in the cause of national defense.

In the face of great perils never before encountered, our strong purpose is to protect and to perpetuate the integrity of democracy.

For this we muster the spirit of America, and the faith of America.

We do not retreat. We are not content to stand still. As Americans, we go forward, in the service of our country, by the will of God.

An American tank passes the Arc de Triomphe after the liberation of Paris, France, August 1944.

INTRODUCTION

F ranklin Roosevelt's decision to run again left no opposition in the Democratic party. The excitement was provided by the choice of vice president. To please southern Democrats who regarded Vice President Henry A. Wallace as too far to the political left, FDR opened the door to Senator Harry S. Truman of Missouri, although he did not entice him directly.

Republican candidate Thomas E. Dewey accused the president of insufficiently supplying the troops in the Pacific theater. He was stunned when just before election day, General MacArthur's forces opened their long-awaited invasion of the Philippine Islands.

Because of the war, the inauguration was held at the White House out of fear of the dangers that might arise in a large crowd. Also, Roosevelt's declining health made a less-exhausting ceremony desirable. About two hundred people were invited; the only ones the president specifically requested were his thirteen grandchildren.

The speech—delivered as the president's son James, in his Marine uniform, stood beside him—was the first inaugural in the tone of a political address with its opening words and acknowledgment of both the chief justice and the new vice president. Also unique was the personal reference to a boyhood hero, Endicott Peabody, formerly headmaster of Groton, FDR's secondary school, and the minister who forty years earlier had performed his marriage to Eleanor.

Franklin Delano Roosevelt
Fourth Inaugural Address

Saturday, January 20, 1945

Mr. Chief Justice, Mr. Vice President,[1] my friends, you will understand and, I believe, agree with my wish that the form of this inauguration be simple and its words brief.

We Americans of today, together with our allies, are passing through a period of supreme test. It is a test of our courage—of our resolve—of our wisdom—our essential democracy.

If we meet that test—successfully and honorably—we shall perform a service of historic importance which men and women and children will honor throughout all time.

As I stand here today, having taken the solemn oath of office in the presence of my fellow countrymen—in the presence of our God—I know that it is America's purpose that we shall not fail.

In the days and in the years that are to come we shall work for a just and honorable peace, a durable peace, as today we work and fight for total victory in war.

---

1. This was the first time that a president acknowledged prominent people on the platform: Harlan Fiske Stone (1872–1946), chief justice of the United States, 1941–46; Harry S. Truman (1884–1972), thirty-fourth vice president, 1945.

President Franklin and Eleanor Roosevelt pose with their thirteen grandchildren at the White House on inauguration day, January 20, 1945.

We can and we will achieve such a peace.

We shall strive for perfection. We shall not achieve it immediately—but we still shall strive. We may make mistakes—but they must never be mistakes which result from faintness of heart or abandonment of moral principle.

I remember that my old schoolmaster, Dr. Peabody,[2] said, in days that seemed to us then to be secure and untroubled: "Things in life will not always run smoothly. Sometimes we will be rising toward the heights—then all will seem to reverse itself and start downward. The great fact to remember is that the trend of civilization itself is forever upward; that a line drawn through the middle of the peaks and the valleys of the centuries always has an upward trend."

Our Constitution of 1787 was not a perfect instrument; it is not perfect yet. But it provided a firm base upon which all manner of men, of all races and colors and creeds, could build our solid structure of democracy.

And so today, in this year of war, 1945, we have learned lessons—at a fearful cost—and we shall profit by them.

We have learned that we cannot live alone, at peace; that our own well-being is dependent on the

---

2. Dr. Endicott Peabody (1857–1944), founder and headmaster of Groton School.

President Franklin Roosevelt (center), English Prime Minister Winston Churchill (left) and Soviet Premier Josef Stalin (right) meet at the Yalta (Crimea) Conference, February 9, 1945.

U.S. Marines raise the American flag on Iwo Jima, one of Japan's outer islands, February 23, 1945. Photograph by Joe Rosenthal.

well-being of other nations far away. We have learned that we must live as men, not as ostriches, nor as dogs in the manger.

We have learned to be citizens of the world, members of the human community.

We have learned the simple truth, as Emerson said, that "The only way to have a friend is to be one."[3] We can gain no lasting peace if we approach it with suspicion and mistrust or with fear.

We can gain it only if we proceed with the understanding, the confidence, and the courage which flow from conviction.

The Almighty God has blessed our land in many ways. He has given our people stout hearts and strong arms with which to strike mighty blows for freedom and truth. He has given to our country a faith which has become the hope of all peoples in an anguished world.

So we pray to Him now for the vision to see our way clearly—to see the way that leads to a better life for ourselves and for all our fellow men—to the achievement of His will to peace on earth.

---

3. Ralph Waldo Emerson (1803–82), American essayist and poet, *Essays, First Series,* 1841.

Harry S. Truman

33rd President of the United States
1945–53

Harry S. Truman

BORN: May 8, 1884, Lamar, Mo.
MARRIED: Elizabeth Virginia "Bess" Wallace, June 28, 1919; one child
DIED: December 26, 1972, Kansas City, Mo.
PARTY: Democratic
EDUCATION: Public schools; attended Kansas City (Mo.) Law School (1923–25).

CAREER:
Captain, Missouri National Guard field artillery, World War I; haberdasher (1919–22) in Independence, Mo.; judge, Jackson County Court (1922–24); presiding judge (1921–34); U.S. Senate (1935–45); vice president (1945); president (1945–53); retired to Independence.

PRESIDENTIAL CAMPAIGNS:
1945: Became president upon Roosevelt's death.
1948: Truman captured the public's affection with a train tour of the country. Badly designed public opinion polls predicted repeat challenger Thomas Dewey the easy winner. But with running-mate Kentucky Senator Alben Barkley, Truman took 57 percent of the vote.
1952: Eligible to run again as the Twenty-second Amendment to the U.S. Constitution, limiting terms of the president, did not apply in his situation, but chose to retire.

Newly elected President Truman gleefully displays the November 3, 1948, Chicago Daily Tribune with headline erroneously announcing his defeat by challenger Thomas Dewey.

Introduction

A shaken Harry Truman said the day after Roosevelt's death: "When they told me yesterday what had happened, I felt like the moon, the stars, and all the planets had fallen on me." He urged the cabinet to stay in place and promised to continue FDR's policies.

In a short time, Truman showed himself to be a strong leader in his own right. Almost immediately he was informed of the nation's most secret military project, the construction of a nuclear weapon. An artillery man in World War I, he regarded the new weapon as simply another form of artillery. Convinced that Japanese leaders would never surrender unless Allied troops actually invaded the Japanese islands, Truman authorized the dropping of an atomic bomb on the city of Hiroshima. The resulting explosion leveled the city and killed tens of thousands of people. When surrender did not result, another nuclear bomb plummeted on Nagasaki, leading finally to the capitulation ordered by the emperor of Japan. Truman explained his actions as done "in order to save the lives of thousands and thousands of young Americans."

The optimistic inaugural address foreshadowed the post-war foreign policy of the United States, including especially the president's "point four," promising aid to the underdeveloped parts of the world.

Harry S. Truman
Inaugural Address

Thursday, January 20, 1949

Mr. Vice President, Mr. Chief Justice,[1] and fellow citizens, I accept with humility the honor which the American people have conferred upon me. I accept it with a deep resolve to do all that I can for the welfare of this nation and for the peace of the world.

In performing the duties of my office, I need the help and prayers of every one of you. I ask for your encouragement and your support. The tasks we face are difficult, and we can accomplish them only if we work together.

Each period of our national history has had its special challenges. Those that confront us now are as momentous as any in the past. Today marks the beginning not only of a new administration, but of a period that will be eventful, perhaps decisive, for us and for the world.

It may be our lot to experience, and in large measure to bring about, a major turning point in the long history of the human race. The first half of this century has been marked by unprecedented

---

1. Alben William Barkley (1877–1956), thirty-fifth vice president, 1949–53; Frederick Moore Vinson (1890–1953), chief justice of the United States, 1946–53.

Smoke billows 20,000 feet over Hiroshima, Japan, after the U.S. Air Force dropped an atomic bomb on the city, August 6, 1945.

and brutal attacks on the rights of man, and by the two most frightful wars in history. The supreme need of our time is for men to learn to live together in peace and harmony.

The peoples of the earth face the future with grave uncertainty, composed almost equally of great hopes and great fears. In this time of doubt, they look to the United States as never before for good will, strength, and wise leadership.

It is fitting, therefore, that we take this occasion to proclaim to the world the essential principles of the faith by which we live, and to declare our aims to all peoples.

The American people stand firm in the faith which has inspired this nation from the beginning. We believe that all men have a right to equal justice under law and equal opportunity to share in the common good. We believe that all men have the right to freedom of thought and expression. We believe that all men are created equal because they are created in the image of God.

From this faith we will not be moved.

The American people desire, and are determined to work for, a world in which all nations and all peoples are free to govern themselves as they see fit, and to achieve a decent and satisfying life. Above all else, our people desire, and are determined to work for, peace on earth—a just and lasting peace—based on genuine agreement freely arrived at by equals.

In the pursuit of these aims, the United States and other like-minded nations find themselves directly opposed by a regime with contrary aims and a totally different concept of life.

That regime adheres to a false philosophy which purports to offer freedom, security, and greater opportunity to mankind. Misled by this philosophy, many peoples have sacrificed their liberties only to learn to their sorrow that deceit and mockery, poverty and tyranny, are their reward.

That false philosophy is communism.

Communism is based on the belief that man is so weak and inadequate that he is unable to govern himself, and therefore requires the rule of strong masters.

Democracy is based on the conviction that man has the moral and intellectual capacity, as well as the inalienable right, to govern himself with reason and justice.

Communism subjects the individual to arrest without lawful cause, punishment without trial, and forced labor as the chattel of the state. It decrees what information he shall receive, what art he shall produce, what leaders he shall follow, and what thoughts he shall think.

Democracy maintains that government is established for the benefit of the individual, and is charged with the responsibility of protecting the rights of the individual and his freedom in the exercise of his abilities.

*In Times Square, a sailor and a nurse celebrate Japan's surrender
and the end of World War II, New York City, August 14, 1945.
Photograph by Lt. Victor Jorgensen.*

179

Communism maintains that social wrongs can be corrected only by violence.

Democracy has proved that social justice can be achieved through peaceful change.

Communism holds that the world is so deeply divided into opposing classes that war is inevitable.

Democracy holds that free nations can settle differences justly and maintain lasting peace.

These differences between communism and democracy do not concern the United States alone. People everywhere are coming to realize that what is involved is material well-being, human dignity, and the right to believe in and worship God.

I state these differences, not to draw issues of belief as such, but because the actions resulting from the Communist philosophy are a threat to the efforts of free nations to bring about world recovery and lasting peace.

Since the end of hostilities, the United States has invested its substance and its energy in a great constructive effort to restore peace, stability, and freedom to the world.

We have sought no territory and we have imposed our will on none. We have asked for no privileges we would not extend to others.

We have constantly and vigorously supported the United Nations[2] and related agencies as a means of

2. The United Nations, post–World War II successor to the League of Nations, was established on October 24, 1945, by fifty-one

applying democratic principles to international relations. We have consistently advocated and relied upon peaceful settlement of disputes among nations.

We have made every effort to secure agreement on effective international control of our most powerful weapon, and we have worked steadily for the limitation and control of all armaments.

We have encouraged, by precept and example, the expansion of world trade on a sound and fair basis.

Almost a year ago, in company with sixteen free nations of Europe, we launched the greatest cooperative economic program in history.[3] The purpose of that unprecedented effort is to invigorate and strengthen democracy in Europe, so that the free people of that continent can resume their rightful place in the forefront of civilization and can contribute once more to the security and welfare of the world.

Our efforts have brought new hope to all mankind. We have beaten back despair and defeatism.

---

countries committed to preserving peace through international cooperation and collective security.

3. The Foreign Assistance Act of 1948 implemented the European Recovery Program, better known as The Marshall Plan, named for its proponent, Secretary of State George Catlett Marshall (1880–1959). The plan had two major aims: to prevent the spread of communism in Western Europe and to stabilize the international order in a way favorable to the development of political democracy and free-market economies.

We have saved a number of countries from losing their liberty. Hundreds of millions of people all over the world now agree with us, that we need not have war—that we can have peace.

The initiative is ours.

We are moving on with other nations to build an even stronger structure of international order and justice. We shall have as our partners countries which, no longer solely concerned with the problem of national survival, are now working to improve the standards of living of all their people. We are ready to undertake new projects to strengthen the free world.

In the coming years, our program for peace and freedom will emphasize four major courses of action.

First, we will continue to give unfaltering support to the United Nations and related agencies, and we will continue to search for ways to strengthen their authority and increase their effectiveness. We believe that the United Nations will be strengthened by the new nations which are being formed in lands now advancing toward self-government under democratic principles.

Second, we will continue our programs for world economic recovery.

This means, first of all, that we must keep our full weight behind the European recovery program. We are confident of the success of this major venture in world recovery. We believe that our partners

Berliners watch a U.S. Air Force C–54 Skymaster land with supplies during the Soviet blockade of the German city in 1948.

in this effort will achieve the status of self-supporting nations once again.

In addition, we must carry out our plans for reducing the barriers to world trade and increasing its volume. Economic recovery and peace itself depend on increased world trade.

Third, we will strengthen freedom-loving nations against the dangers of aggression.

We are now working out with a number of countries a joint agreement designed to strengthen the security of the North Atlantic area.[4] Such an agreement would take the form of a collective defense arrangement within the terms of the United Nations Charter.

We have already established such a defense pact for the Western Hemisphere by the treaty of Rio de Janeiro.[5]

The primary purpose of these agreements is to provide unmistakable proof of the joint determination of the free countries to resist armed attack from any quarter. Each country participating in these arrangements must contribute all it can to the common defense.

4. North Atlantic Treaty, signed by twelve nations, April 4, 1949. The North Atlantic Treaty Organization (NATO) was created to carry out agreements based on security guarantees and mutual commitments between Europe and North America.
5. Inter-American Treaty of Reciprocal Assistance, Rio de Janeiro, Brazil, September 2, 1947, was intended to prevent and repel threats and acts of aggression against any of the countries of America.

If we can make it sufficiently clear, in advance, that any armed attack affecting our national security would be met with overwhelming force, the armed attack might never occur.

I hope soon to send to the Senate a treaty respecting the North Atlantic security plan.

In addition, we will provide military advice and equipment to free nations which will cooperate with us in the maintenance of peace and security.

Fourth, we must embark on a bold new program for making the benefits of our scientific advances and industrial progress available for the improvement and growth of underdeveloped areas.

More than half the people of the world are living in conditions approaching misery. Their food is inadequate. They are victims of disease. Their economic life is primitive and stagnant. Their poverty is a handicap and a threat both to them and to more prosperous areas.

For the first time in history, humanity possesses the knowledge and the skill to relieve the suffering of these people.

The United States is pre-eminent among nations in the development of industrial and scientific techniques. The material resources which we can afford to use for the assistance of other peoples are limited. But our imponderable resources in technical knowledge are constantly growing and are inexhaustible.

I believe that we should make available to peace-loving peoples the benefits of our store of technical knowledge in order to help them realize their aspirations for a better life. And, in cooperation with other nations, we should foster capital investment in areas needing development.

Our aim should be to help the free peoples of the world, through their own efforts, to produce more food, more clothing, more materials for housing, and more mechanical power to lighten their burdens.

We invite other countries to pool their technological resources in this undertaking. Their contributions will be warmly welcomed. This should be a cooperative enterprise in which all nations work together through the United Nations and its specialized agencies wherever practicable. It must be a worldwide effort for the achievement of peace, plenty, and freedom.

With the cooperation of business, private capital, agriculture, and labor in this country, this program can greatly increase the industrial activity in other nations and can raise substantially their standards of living.

Such new economic developments must be devised and controlled to benefit the peoples of the areas in which they are established. Guarantees to the investor must be balanced by guarantees in the interest of the people whose resources and whose labor go into these developments.

The old imperialism—exploitation for foreign

President Truman meets General Douglas MacArthur, whom he would later relieve of command, on Wake Island in the Pacific, October 14, 1950.

profit—has no place in our plans. What we envisage is a program of development based on the concepts of democratic fair-dealing.

All countries, including our own, will greatly benefit from a constructive program for the better use of the world's human and natural resources. Experience shows that our commerce with other countries expands as they progress industrially and economically.

Greater production is the key to prosperity and peace. And the key to greater production is a wider and more vigorous application of modern scientific and technical knowledge.

Only by helping the least fortunate of its members to help themselves can the human family achieve the decent, satisfying life that is the right of all people.

Democracy alone can supply the vitalizing force to stir the peoples of the world into triumphant action, not only against their human oppressors, but also against their ancient enemies—hunger, misery, and despair.

On the basis of these four major courses of action we hope to help create the conditions that will lead eventually to personal freedom and happiness for all mankind.

If we are to be successful in carrying out these policies, it is clear that we must have continued prosperity in this country and we must keep ourselves strong.

Slowly but surely we are weaving a world fabric of international security and growing prosperity.

We are aided by all who wish to live in freedom from fear—even by those who live today in fear under their own governments.

We are aided by all who want relief from the lies of propaganda—who desire truth and sincerity.

We are aided by all who desire self-government and a voice in deciding their own affairs.

We are aided by all who long for economic security—for the security and abundance that men in free societies can enjoy.

We are aided by all who desire freedom of speech, freedom of religion, and freedom to live their own lives for useful ends.

Our allies are the millions who hunger and thirst after righteousness.

In due time, as our stability becomes manifest, as more and more nations come to know the benefits of democracy and to participate in growing abundance, I believe that those countries which now oppose us will abandon their delusions and join with the free nations of the world in a just settlement of international differences.

Events have brought our American democracy to new influence and new responsibilities. They will test our courage, our devotion to duty, and our concept of liberty.

But I say to all men, what we have achieved in liberty, we will surpass in greater liberty.

Steadfast in our faith in the Almighty, we

will advance toward a world where man's freedom is secure.

To that end we will devote our strength, our resources, and our firmness of resolve. With God's help, the future of mankind will be assured in a world of justice, harmony, and peace.

Dwight David Eisenhower

34th President of the United States
1953–61

Dwight David Eisenhower

BORN: October 14, 1890, Denison, Texas
MARRIED: Marie Geneva "Mamie" Doud, July 1,
1916; two children
DIED: March 28, 1969, Washington, D.C.
PARTY: Republican
EDUCATION: Public schools, Abilene, Kans.; U.S.
Military Academy (1915); Command and General Staff
School (1925–26); Army War College (1928–29).

CAREER:
Career Army: World War I at Fort Sam Houston, Texas;
Panama Canal Zone (1922–24); rose to senior positions;
commander of U.S. forces in Europe (1942); commander in chief of Allied invasions of North Africa,
Sicily, and Italy; supreme Allied commander for invasion of Europe (1943–45); chief of staff (1945–48);
retired from active duty (1948). President, Columbia
University (1948–50); supreme commander of the
North Atlantic Treaty Organization Forces in Europe
(1950–52); resigned to run for president; president
(1953–61); retired to Gettysburg, Pa.

PRESIDENTIAL CAMPAIGNS:
1952: Ran with California Senator Richard M. Nixon.
Elected by a huge margin over Democratic Governor
Adlai E. Stevenson of Illinois.
1956: Beat Stevenson again by an even larger margin.

*January 20, 1957, fell on a Sunday, so President Eisenhower
took his second oath of office in a private ceremony in the East Room
of the White House.*

INTRODUCTION

D wight Eisenhower ran for president in the great
tradition of the country's victorious generals:
Washington, Jackson, Taylor, and Grant. Wooed after
World War II by both parties, Eisenhower shunned
politics, serving as president of Columbia University.
In 1950, President Truman sent him to command the
North Atlantic Treaty Organization's forces as the cold
war against the Soviet Union commenced.

By 1952, Republicans lured Eisenhower as their candidate. Although his campaign was regarded as uninspiring, the public really did not look for a program
from him. They enjoyed his smile and willingly wore
his campaign button reading simply: "I like Ike."

Truman and Eisenhower did not get along. Eisenhower seemed infuriated that Truman had Eisenhower's surviving son, John, brought home for the
inauguration from Korea. Ike feared this high-level
favoritism would damage his son's military career. The
two presidents did not make up until Kennedy's
funeral in 1963.

The inaugural address, which is unimaginative
and organized like a committee report, does not reflect
the new president's considerable gifts as a writer. Ike
set the fashion by wearing a homburg hat and set the
tone by preceding the address with a prayer that he
said he had written that morning after church.

Dwight David Eisenhower
First Inaugural Address

Tuesday, January 20, 1953

My friends, before I begin the expression of those thoughts that I deem appropriate to this moment, would you permit me the privilege of uttering a little private prayer of my own. And I ask that you bow your heads:

Almighty God, as we stand here at this moment my future associates in the Executive branch of government join me in beseeching that Thou will make full and complete our dedication to the service of the people in this throng, and their fellow citizens everywhere.

Give us, we pray, the power to discern clearly right from wrong, and allow all our words and actions to be governed thereby, and by the laws of this land. Especially we pray that our concern shall be for all the people regardless of station, race, or calling.

May cooperation be permitted and be the mutual aim of those who, under the concepts of our Constitution, hold to differing political faiths; so that all may work for the good of our beloved country and Thy glory. Amen.

My fellow citizens:

The world and we have passed the midway point of a century of continuing challenge. We sense with all our faculties that forces of good and evil are massed and armed and opposed as rarely before in history.

This fact defines the meaning of this day. We are summoned by this honored and historic ceremony to witness more than the act of one citizen swearing his oath of service, in the presence of God. We are called as a people to give testimony in the sight of the world to our faith that the future shall belong to the free.

Since this century's beginning, a time of tempest has seemed to come upon the continents of the earth. Masses of Asia have awakened to strike off shackles of the past. Great nations of Europe have fought their bloodiest wars. Thrones have toppled and their vast empires have disappeared. New nations have been born.

For our own country, it has been a time of recurring trial. We have grown in power and in responsibility. We have passed through the anxieties of depression and of war to a summit unmatched in man's history. Seeking to secure peace in the world, we have had to fight through the forests of the Argonne, to the shores of Iwo Jima, and to the cold mountains of Korea.

In the swift rush of great events, we find ourselves groping to know the full sense and meaning of these times in which we live. In our quest of understanding, we beseech God's guidance. We

*As promised in his campaign, President-elect Eisenhower visits the
First Republic of Korea before his inauguration day. Capitol
Division headquarters, December 4, 1952.*

summon all our knowledge of the past and we scan all signs of the future. We bring all our wit and all our will to meet the question:

How far have we come in man's long pilgrimage from darkness toward light? Are we nearing the light—a day of freedom and of peace for all mankind? Or are the shadows of another night closing in upon us?

Great as are the preoccupations absorbing us at home, concerned as we are with matters that deeply affect our livelihood today and our vision of the future, each of these domestic problems is dwarfed by, and often even created by, this question that involves all humankind.

This trial comes at a moment when man's power to achieve good or to inflict evil surpasses the brightest hopes and the sharpest fears of all ages. We can turn rivers in their courses, level mountains to the plains. Oceans and land and sky are avenues for our colossal commerce. Disease diminishes and life lengthens.

Yet the promise of this life is imperiled by the very genius that has made it possible. Nations amass wealth. Labor sweats to create—and turns out devices to level not only mountains but also cities. Science seems ready to confer upon us, as its final gift, the power to erase human life from this planet.

At such a time in history, we who are free must proclaim anew our faith. This faith is the abiding creed of our fathers. It is our faith in the deathless dignity of man, governed by eternal moral and natural laws.

This faith defines our full view of life. It establishes, beyond debate, those gifts of the Creator that are man's inalienable rights, and that make all men equal in His sight.

In the light of this equality, we know that the virtues most cherished by free people—love of truth, pride of work, devotion to country—all are treasures equally precious in the lives of the most humble and of the most exalted. The men who mine coal and fire furnaces and balance ledgers and turn lathes and pick cotton and heal the sick and plant corn—all serve as proudly, and as profitably, for America as the statesmen who draft treaties and the legislators who enact laws.

This faith rules our whole way of life. It decrees that we, the people, elect leaders not to rule but to serve. It asserts that we have the right to choice of our own work and to the reward of our own toil. It inspires the initiative that makes our productivity the wonder of the world. And it warns that any man who seeks to deny equality among all his brothers betrays the spirit of the free and invites the mockery of the tyrant.

It is because we, all of us, hold to these principles that the political changes accomplished this day do not imply turbulence, upheaval or disorder. Rather this change expresses a purpose of strengthening our dedication and devotion to the precepts of our founding documents, a conscious renewal of faith in our country and in the watchfulness of a Divine Providence.

The enemies of this faith know no god but force, no devotion but its use. They tutor men in treason. They feed upon the hunger of others. Whatever defies them, they torture, especially the truth.

Here, then, is joined no argument between slightly differing philosophies. This conflict strikes directly at the faith of our fathers and the lives of our sons. No principle or treasure that we hold, from the spiritual knowledge of our free schools and churches to the creative magic of free labor and capital, nothing lies safely beyond the reach of this struggle.

Freedom is pitted against slavery; lightness against the dark.

The faith we hold belongs not to us alone but to the free of all the world. This common bond binds the grower of rice in Burma and the planter of wheat in Iowa, the shepherd in southern Italy and the mountaineer in the Andes. It confers a common dignity upon the French soldier who dies in Indo-China, the British soldier killed in Malaya, the American life given in Korea.

We know, beyond this, that we are linked to all free peoples not merely by a noble idea but by a simple need. No free people can for long cling to any privilege or enjoy any safety in economic solitude. For all our own material might, even we need markets in the world for the surpluses of our farms and our factories. Equally, we need for these same farms and factories vital materials and products of distant lands. This basic law of interdependence, so manifest in the commerce of peace, applies with thousand-fold intensity in the event of war.

So we are persuaded by necessity and by belief that the strength of all free peoples lies in unity; their danger, in discord.

To produce this unity, to meet the challenge of our time, destiny has laid upon our country the responsibility of the free world's leadership.

So it is proper that we assure our friends once again that, in the discharge of this responsibility, we Americans know and we observe the difference between world leadership and imperialism; between firmness and truculence; between a thoughtfully calculated goal and spasmodic reaction to the stimulus of emergencies.

We wish our friends the world over to know this above all: we face the threat—not with dread and confusion—but with confidence and conviction.

We feel this moral strength because we know that we are not helpless prisoners of history. We are free men. We shall remain free, never to be proven guilty of the one capital offense against freedom, a lack of stanch faith.

In pleading our just cause before the bar of history and in pressing our labor for world peace, we shall be guided by certain fixed principles.

These principles are:

(1) Abhorring war as a chosen way to balk the purposes of those who threaten us, we hold it to be the first task of statesmanship to develop the strength that will deter the forces of aggression and promote the conditions of peace. For, as it must be the supreme purpose of all free men, so it must be the dedication of their leaders, to save humanity from preying upon itself.

In the light of this principle, we stand ready to engage with any and all others in joint effort to remove the causes of mutual fear and distrust among nations, so as to make possible drastic reduction of armaments. The sole requisites for undertaking such effort are that—in their purpose—they be aimed logically and honestly toward secure peace for all; and that—in their result—they provide methods by which every participating nation will prove good faith in carrying out its pledge.

(2) Realizing that common sense and common decency alike dictate the futility of appeasement, we shall never try to placate an aggressor by the false and wicked bargain of trading honor for security. Americans, indeed all free men, remember that in the final choice a soldier's pack is not so heavy a burden as a prisoner's chains.

(3) Knowing that only a United States that is strong and immensely productive can help defend freedom in our world, we view our Nation's strength and security as a trust upon which rests the hope of free men everywhere. It is the firm duty of each of our free citizens and of every free citizen everywhere to place the cause of his country before the comfort, the convenience of himself.

(4) Honoring the identity and the special heritage of each nation in the world, we shall never use our strength to try to impress upon another people our own cherished political and economic institutions.

(5) Assessing realistically the needs and capacities of proven friends of freedom, we shall strive to help them to achieve their own security and well-being. Likewise, we shall count upon them to assume, within the limits of their resources, their full and just burdens in the common defense of freedom.

(6) Recognizing economic health as an indispensable basis of military strength and the free world's peace, we shall strive to foster everywhere, and to practice ourselves, policies that encourage productivity and profitable trade. For the impoverishment of any single people in the world means danger to the well-being of all other peoples.

(7) Appreciating that economic need, military security and political wisdom combine to suggest regional groupings of free peoples, we hope, within the framework of the United Nations, to help

strengthen such special bonds the world over. The nature of these ties must vary with the different problems of different areas.

In the Western Hemisphere, we enthusiastically join with all our neighbors in the work of perfecting a community of fraternal trust and common purpose.

In Europe, we ask that enlightened and inspired leaders of the western nations strive with renewed vigor to make the unity of their peoples a reality. Only as free Europe unitedly marshals its strength can it effectively safeguard, even with our help, its spiritual and cultural heritage.

(8) Conceiving the defense of freedom, like freedom itself, to be one and indivisible, we hold all continents and peoples in equal regard and honor. We reject any insinuation that one race or another, one people or another, is in any sense inferior or expendable.

(9) Respecting the United Nations as the living sign of all people's hope for peace, we shall strive to make it not merely an eloquent symbol but an effective force. And in our quest for an honorable peace, we shall neither compromise, nor tire, nor ever cease.

By these rules of conduct, we hope to be known to all peoples.

By their observance, an earth of peace may become not a vision but a fact.

This hope—this supreme aspiration—must rule the way we live.

We must be ready to dare all for our country. For history does not long entrust the care of freedom to the weak or the timid. We must acquire proficiency in defense and display stamina in purpose.

We must be willing, individually and as a Nation, to accept whatever sacrifices may be required of us. A people that values its privileges above its principles soon loses both.

These basic precepts are not lofty abstractions, far removed from matters of daily living. They are laws of spiritual strength that generate and define our material strength. Patriotism means equipped forces and a prepared citizenry. Moral stamina means more energy and more productivity, on the farm and in the factory. Love of liberty means the guarding of every resource that makes freedom possible—from the sanctity of our families and the wealth of our soil to the genius of our scientists.

And so each citizen plays an indispensable role. The productivity of our heads, our hands, and our hearts is the source of all the strength we can command, for both the enrichment of our lives and the winning of the peace.

No person, no home, no community can be beyond the reach of this call. We are summoned to act in wisdom and in conscience, to work with industry, to teach with persuasion, to preach with convic-

U.S. civil defense poster issued in 1954 during height of cold war-era fears of nuclear attack.

tion, to weigh our every deed with care and with compassion. For this truth must be clear before us: whatever America hopes to bring to pass in the world must first come to pass in the heart of America.

The peace we seek, then, is nothing less than the practice and fulfillment of our whole faith among ourselves and in our dealings with others. This signifies more than the stilling of guns, easing the sorrow of war. More than escape from death, it is a way of life. More than a haven for the weary, it is a hope for the brave.

This is the hope that beckons us onward in this century of trial. This is the work that awaits us all, to be done with bravery, with charity, and with prayer to Almighty God.

INTRODUCTION

D wight Eisenhower was an ailing man when he decided to run again. During his first term he had suffered a moderately severe heart seizure and also had serious colon surgery for ileitis. He had, however, already demonstrated that his military experience taught him to rely heavily on his staff's work.

The public appreciated him not as a man introducing new programs, but as an avuncular figure above the nit-picking ways of politicians. Now many historians see his regime as a "hidden-hand presidency," which allowed him to appear passive while actively pressing for his political policies.

January 20, 1957, fell on a Sunday; thus, Ike took his second oath of office privately in the East Room of the White House. Eighty people—mostly family and close friends—were present. The press was not invited.

The next day, Eisenhower was sworn in publicly by Chief Justice Earl Warren. Eisenhower had appointed him to the Supreme Court but now regarded Warren's liberal decisions as proof he had made a mistake.

Eisenhower delivered a much stronger speech than his first. In saying that the nation must be prepared to pay any price to keep the peace, he seemed to assail the Republican party's position on government spending. Already the president was relying more on the cooperation of the Senate Majority Leader Lyndon B. Johnson than on the Republican leadership in Congress.

Dwight David Eisenhower
Second Inaugural Address

Monday, January 21, 1957

The Price of Peace

Mr. Chairman, Mr. Vice President, Mr. Chief Justice, Mr. Speaker,[1] members of my family and friends, my countrymen, and the friends of my country, wherever they may be, we meet again, as upon a like moment four years ago, and again you have witnessed my solemn oath of service to you.

I, too, am a witness, today testifying in your name to the principles and purposes to which we, as a people, are pledged.

Before all else, we seek, upon our common labor as a nation, the blessings of Almighty God. And the hopes in our hearts fashion the deepest prayers of our whole people.

May we pursue the right—without self-righteousness.

May we know unity—without conformity.

May we grow in strength—without pride in self.

---

1. Senator Henry Stiles Bridges (1898–1961) (R–NH), 1937–62, chairman of the Joint Congressional Committee; Richard Milhous Nixon (1913–94), thirty-sixth vice president, 1953–61; Earl Warren (1891–1969), chief justice of the United States, 1953–69; Congressman Samuel Taliaferro Rayburn (1882–1961) (D–TX), 1913–61, Speaker of the House of Representatives, 1939–46, 1949–52, 1955–61.

May we, in our dealings with all peoples of the earth, ever speak truth and serve justice.

And so shall America—in the sight of all men of good will—prove true to the honorable purposes that bind and rule us as a people in all this time of trial through which we pass.

We live in a land of plenty, but rarely has this earth known such peril as today.

In our nation work and wealth abound. Our population grows. Commerce crowds our rivers and rails, our skies, harbors, and highways. Our soil is fertile, our agriculture productive. The air rings with the song of our industry—rolling mills and blast furnaces, dynamos, dams, and assembly lines—the chorus of America the bountiful.

This is our home—yet this is not the whole of our world. For our world is where our full destiny lies—with men, of all people, and all nations, who are or would be free. And for them—and so for us—this is no time of ease or of rest.

In too much of the earth there is want, discord, danger. New forces and new nations stir and strive across the earth, with power to bring, by their fate, great good or great evil to the free world's future. From the deserts of North Africa to the islands of the South Pacific one third of all mankind has entered upon an historic struggle for a new freedom; freedom from grinding poverty. Across all continents, nearly a billion people seek, sometimes almost in despera-

Families line up in the Protection, Kansas, high school gym to immunize children against polio with the newly developed Salk vaccine, 1957.

tion, for the skills and knowledge and assistance by which they may satisfy from their own resources, the material wants common to all mankind.

No nation, however old or great, escapes this tempest of change and turmoil. Some, impoverished by the recent World War, seek to restore their means of livelihood. In the heart of Europe, Germany still stands tragically divided. So is the whole continent divided. And so, too, is all the world.

The divisive force is International Communism and the power that it controls.

The designs of that power, dark in purpose, are clear in practice. It strives to seal forever the fate of those it has enslaved. It strives to break the ties that unite the free. And it strives to capture—to exploit for its own greater power—all forces of change in the world, especially the needs of the hungry and the hopes of the oppressed.

Yet the world of International Communism has itself been shaken by a fierce and mighty force: the readiness of men who love freedom to pledge their lives to that love. Through the night of their bondage, the unconquerable will of heroes has struck with the swift, sharp thrust of lightning. Budapest is no longer merely the name of a city; henceforth it is a new and shining symbol of man's yearning to be free.[2]

---

2. Refers to the Hungarian uprising of 1956, which was quelled by Soviet tanks.

Freedom fighters wave the Hungarian flag from a captured Soviet tank in front of the parliament building in Budapest, November 2, 1956.

Thus across all the globe there harshly blow the winds of change. And, we—though fortunate be our lot—know that we can never turn our backs to them.

We look upon this shaken earth, and we declare our firm and fixed purpose—the building of a peace with justice in a world where moral law prevails.

The building of such a peace is a bold and solemn purpose. To proclaim it is easy. To serve it will be hard. And to attain it, we must be aware of its full meaning—and ready to pay its full price.

We know clearly what we seek, and why.

We seek peace, knowing that peace is the climate of freedom. And now, as in no other age, we seek it because we have been warned, by the power of modern weapons, that peace may be the only climate possible for human life itself.

Yet this peace we seek cannot be born of fear alone: it must be rooted in the lives of nations. There must be justice, sensed and shared by all peoples, for, without justice the world can know only a tense and unstable truce. There must be law, steadily invoked and respected by all nations, for without law, the world promises only such meager justice as the pity of the strong upon the weak. But the law of which we speak, comprehending the values of freedom, affirms the equality of all nations, great and small.

Splendid as can be the blessings of such a peace, high will be its cost: in toil patiently sustained, in help honorably given, in sacrifice calmly borne.

We are called to meet the price of this peace.

To counter the threat of those who seek to rule by force, we must pay the costs of our own needed military strength, and help to build the security of others.

We must use our skills and knowledge and, at times, our substance, to help others rise from misery, however far the scene of suffering may be from our shores. For wherever in the world a people knows desperate want, there must appear at least the spark of hope, the hope of progress—or there will surely rise at last the flames of conflict.

We recognize and accept our own deep involvement in the destiny of men everywhere. We are accordingly pledged to honor, and to strive to fortify, the authority of the United Nations. For in that body rests the best hope of our age for the assertion of that law by which all nations may live in dignity.

And, beyond this general resolve, we are called to act a responsible role in the world's great concerns or conflicts—whether they touch upon the affairs of a vast region, the fate of an island in the Pacific, or the use of a canal in the Middle East. Only in respecting the hopes and cultures of others will we practice the equality of all nations. Only as we show willingness and wisdom in giving counsel—in receiving counsel—and in sharing burdens, will we wisely perform the work of peace.

For one truth must rule all we think and all we do. No people can live to itself alone. The unity of all who dwell in freedom is their only sure defense. The economic need of all nations—in mutual dependence—makes isolation an impossibility; not even America's prosperity could long survive if other nations did not also prosper. No nation can longer be a fortress, lone and strong and safe. And any people, seeking such shelter for themselves, can now build only their own prison.

Our pledge to these principles is constant, because we believe in their rightness.

We do not fear this world of change. America is no stranger to much of its spirit. Everywhere we see the seeds of the same growth that America itself has known. The American experiment has, for generations, fired the passion and the courage of millions elsewhere seeking freedom, equality, and opportunity. And the American story of material progress has helped excite the longing of all needy peoples for some satisfaction of their human wants. These hopes that we have helped to inspire, we can help to fulfill.

In this confidence, we speak plainly to all peoples.

We cherish our friendship with all nations that are or would be free. We respect, no less, their independence. And when, in time of want or peril, they ask our help, they may honorably receive it; for we no more seek to buy their sovereignty than we would sell our own. Sovereignty is never bartered among freemen.

We honor the aspirations of those nations which, now captive, long for freedom. We seek neither

National Guard troops control milling crowd of students, sightseers, and press awaiting attempts by Negro students to register at Central High School, Little Rock, Arkansas, September 5, 1957.

their military alliance nor any artificial imitation of our society. And they can know the warmth of the welcome that awaits them when, as must be, they join again the ranks of freedom.

We honor, no less in this divided world than in a less tormented time, the people of Russia. We do not dread, rather do we welcome, their progress in education and industry. We wish them success in their demands for more intellectual freedom, greater security before their own laws, fuller enjoyment of the rewards of their own toil. For as such things come to pass, the more certain will be the coming of that day when our peoples may freely meet in friendship.

So we voice our hope and our belief that we can help to heal this divided world. Thus may the nations cease to live in trembling before the menace of force. Thus may the weight of fear and the weight of arms be taken from the burdened shoulders of mankind.

This, nothing less, is the labor to which we are called and our strength dedicated.

And so the prayer of our people carries far beyond our own frontiers, to the wide world of our duty and our destiny.

May the light of freedom, coming to all darkened lands, flame brightly—until at last the darkness is no more.

May the turbulence of our age yield to a true time of peace, when men and nations shall share a life that honors the dignity of each, the brotherhood of all.

John Fitzgerald Kennedy
35th President of the United States
1961–63

John Fitzgerald Kennedy

BORN: May 29, 1917, Brookline, Mass.
MARRIED: Jacqueline Lee Bouvier, September 12, 1953; three children
DIED: November 22, 1963, in Dallas, Texas
PARTY: Democratic
EDUCATION: Public and private schools in Brookline, Mass.; Choate School in Wallingford, Conn.; London School of Economics and Princeton University; Harvard College (1940); attended Stanford University School of Business.

CAREER:
U.S. Navy (1941–45): commanded a PT boat that sank in the South Pacific; author and newspaper correspondent (Pulitzer Prize for book, *Profiles in Courage*); U.S. House of Representatives (1947–53); U.S. Senate (1953–60); president (1961–63); assassinated.

PRESIDENTIAL CAMPAIGN:
1960: Kennedy's superiority in first televised presidential debates contributed to a 100,000-vote victory over Republican Richard M. Nixon. Kennedy family presence in the media introduced a new clan to public life. First successful campaign of a Roman Catholic for president was marked by a keen awareness of why Al Smith failed in 1928.

*President-elect Kennedy and his wife, Jacqueline,
leave their Georgetown home for his inauguration,
January 20, 1961.*

Introduction

John Kennedy was forty-three years old, the youngest president ever elected, when he succeeded Eisenhower who, at seventy, was the oldest sitting president. The public saw the shift from age to youth as the sign of a greater shift than usual in the nation's direction. The president-elect's decision to wear a top hat at his oath-taking—not a homburg as Ike had—was a gentle signal that a new time was coming.

Kennedy's heroic role as a naval officer was reassuring evidence that he knew the high cost of war and that, despite the firmness of his words pledging America's commitment to "assure the survival and the success of liberty," he was a man of peace.

The weather on January 19 was a great burden as eight inches of snow fell and roads became impassable. But by inauguration day the snow had stopped and Pennsylvania Avenue had been cleared by workers who had shoveled all night. Still, the wind-chill at noon was zero degrees. Boldly and determinedly, Kennedy attended all five of the inaugural balls in the city, winding up at the party held by his prep-school classmates from the Choate School.

The carefully prepared speech is remembered for many of its resonant phrases. In preparing it, aides had read all previous inaugurals and had determined to produce a superior one.

John Fitzgerald Kennedy
Inaugural Address

Friday, January 20, 1961

Vice President Johnson, Mr. Speaker, Mr. Chief Justice, President Eisenhower, Vice President Nixon, President Truman,[1] reverend clergy, fellow citizens, we observe today not a victory of party, but a celebration of freedom—symbolizing an end, as well as a beginning—signifying renewal, as well as change. For I have sworn before you and Almighty God the same solemn oath our forebears prescribed nearly a century and three quarters ago.

The world is very different now. For man holds in his mortal hands the power to abolish all forms of human poverty and all forms of human life. And yet the same revolutionary beliefs for which our forebears fought are still at issue around the globe— the belief that the rights of man come not from the generosity of the state, but from the hand of God.

We dare not forget today that we are the heirs of that first revolution. Let the word go forth from this

---

1. Lyndon Baines Johnson (1908–73), thirty-seventh vice president, 1961–63; Congressman Samuel Taliaferro Rayburn (1882–1961) (D–TX), 1913–61, Speaker of the House of Representatives, 1939–46, 1949–52, 1955–61; Earl Warren (1891–1974), chief justice of the United States, 1953–69; President Dwight David Eisenhower; Richard Milhous Nixon (1913–94), thirty-sixth vice president, 1953–61; President Harry S. Truman.

time and place, to friend and foe alike, that the torch has been passed to a new generation of Americans—born in this century, tempered by war, disciplined by a hard and bitter peace, proud of our ancient heritage—and unwilling to witness or permit the slow undoing of those human rights to which this nation has always been committed, and to which we are committed today at home and around the world.

Let every nation know, whether it wishes us well or ill, that we shall pay any price, bear any burden, meet any hardship, support any friend, oppose any foe, in order to assure the survival and the success of liberty.

This much we pledge—and more.

To those old allies whose cultural and spiritual origins we share, we pledge the loyalty of faithful friends. United, there is little we cannot do in a host of cooperative ventures. Divided, there is little we can do—for we dare not meet a powerful challenge at odds and split asunder.

To those new states whom we welcome to the ranks of the free, we pledge our word that one form of colonial control shall not have passed away merely to be replaced by a far more iron tyranny. We shall not always expect to find them supporting our view. But we shall always hope to find them strongly supporting their own freedom—and to remember that, in the past, those who foolishly sought power by riding the back of the tiger ended up inside.

To those peoples in the huts and villages across the globe struggling to break the bonds of mass misery, we pledge our best efforts to help them help themselves, for whatever period is required—not because the Communists may be doing it, not because we seek their votes, but because it is right. If a free society cannot help the many who are poor, it cannot save the few who are rich.

To our sister republics south of our border, we offer a special pledge—to convert our good words into good deeds—in a new alliance for progress— to assist free men and free governments in casting off the chains of poverty. But this peaceful revolution of hope cannot become the prey of hostile powers. Let all our neighbors know that we shall join with them to oppose aggression or subversion anywhere in the Americas. And let every other power know that this Hemisphere intends to remain the master of its own house.

To that world assembly of sovereign states, the United Nations, our last best hope in an age where the instruments of war have far outpaced the instruments of peace, we renew our pledge of support—to prevent it from becoming merely a forum for invective—to strengthen its shield of the new and the weak—and to enlarge the area in which its writ may run.

Finally, to those nations who would make themselves our adversary, we offer not a pledge but a request: that both sides begin anew the quest for peace, before the dark powers of destruction unleashed by science engulf all humanity in planned or accidental self-destruction.

We dare not tempt them with weakness. For only when our arms are sufficient beyond doubt can we be certain beyond doubt that they will never be employed.

But neither can two great and powerful groups of nations take comfort from our present course— both sides overburdened by the cost of modern weapons, both rightly alarmed by the steady spread of the deadly atom, yet both racing to alter that uncertain balance of terror that stays the hand of mankind's final war.

So let us begin anew—remembering on both sides that civility is not a sign of weakness, and sincerity is always subject to proof. Let us never negotiate out of fear. But let us never fear to negotiate.

Let both sides explore what problems unite us instead of belaboring those problems which divide us.

Let both sides, for the first time, formulate serious and precise proposals for the inspection and control of arms—and bring the absolute power to destroy other nations under the absolute control of all nations.

Let both sides seek to invoke the wonders of science instead of its terrors. Together let us explore the stars, conquer the deserts, eradicate disease, tap the ocean depths, and encourage the arts and commerce.

The Rev. Martin Luther King Jr., delivers his "I have a dream" speech to the vast crowd gathered at the Lincoln Memorial, Washington, D.C., August 28, 1963.

Let both sides unite to heed in all corners of the earth the command of Isaiah—to "undo the heavy burdens . . . and to let the oppressed go free."[2]

And if a beachhead of cooperation may push back the jungle of suspicion, let both sides join in creating a new endeavor, not a new balance of power, but a new world of law, where the strong are just and the weak secure and the peace preserved.

All this will not be finished in the first 100 days. Nor will it be finished in the first 1,000 days, nor in the life of this Administration, nor even perhaps in our lifetime on this planet. But let us begin.

In your hands, my fellow citizens, more than in mine, will rest the final success or failure of our course. Since this country was founded, each generation of Americans has been summoned to give testimony to its national loyalty. The graves of young Americans who answered the call to service surround the globe.

Now the trumpet summons us again—not as a call to bear arms, though arms we need; not as a call to battle, though embattled we are—but a call to bear the burden of a long twilight struggle, year in and year out, "rejoicing in hope, patient in tribulation"[3]—a struggle against the common enemies of man: tyranny, poverty, disease, and war itself.

---

2. Isaiah 58:6.
3. Romans 12:12 (Epistle of Paul the Apostle to the Romans).

Jacqueline Kennedy, flanked by brothers-in-law Edward and Robert Kennedy and children, Caroline and John Jr., watches her husband's funeral procession, Washington, D.C., November 25, 1963.

Can we forge against these enemies a grand and global alliance, North and South, East and West, that can assure a more fruitful life for all mankind? Will you join in that historic effort?

In the long history of the world, only a few generations have been granted the role of defending freedom in its hour of maximum danger. I do not shrink from this responsibility—I welcome it. I do not believe that any of us would exchange places with any other people or any other generation. The energy, the faith, the devotion which we bring to this endeavor will light our country and all who serve it—and the glow from that fire can truly light the world.

And so, my fellow Americans: ask not what your country can do for you—ask what you can do for your country.

My fellow citizens of the world: ask not what America will do for you, but what together we can do for the freedom of man.

Finally, whether you are citizens of America or citizens of the world, ask of us the same high standards of strength and sacrifice which we ask of you. With a good conscience our only sure reward, with history the final judge of our deeds, let us go forth to lead the land we love, asking His blessing and His help, but knowing that here on earth God's work must truly be our own.

Lyndon Baines Johnson

36th President of the United States
1963–69

Lyndon Baines Johnson

BORN: August 27, 1908, near Stonewall, Texas
MARRIED: Claudia Alta "Lady Bird" Taylor, November 17, 1934; two children
DIED: January 22, 1973, Johnson City, Texas
EDUCATION: Public schools; Southwest Texas State Teachers College (1930); attended Georgetown University Law School (1934).

CAREER:
Teacher (1928–31); congressional aide (1931–35); Texas director, National Youth Administration (1935–37); U.S. House of Representatives (1937–49); first congressman to volunteer after Pearl Harbor: U.S. Navy (1941–42) until ordered back to Congress; U.S. Senate (1949–61); Democratic whip (1951–53); minority leader (1953–55); majority leader (1955–61); vice president (1961–63); president (1963–69); retired to LBJ Ranch in Texas.

PRESIDENTIAL CAMPAIGNS:
1963: Became president on Kennedy's death.
1964: Ran with Minnesota Senator Hubert H. Humphrey against Arizona Senator Barry Goldwater, whose radical conservatism proved fatal. Johnson won 61 percent of the total popular vote—the most ever attained by a presidential candidate.
1968: Did not seek reelection.

As Jacqueline Kennedy and Lady Bird Johnson watch, Judge Sarah Hughes administers the oath of office to Vice President Lyndon Johnson on Air Force One only hours after President Kennedy's assassination in Dallas, Texas, November 22, 1963.

INTRODUCTION

Lyndon Johnson was the first vice president actually present when his predecessor died. On November 22, 1963, he was riding in the motorcade shattered by the assassination of Kennedy in Dallas, Texas. Although eager to leave for Washington and get out of the way of possible further assaults on the country's leaders, Johnson waited until Mrs. Kennedy could board the presidential aircraft. Then, she would not leave without her husband's body. Finally at 2:38 p.m., Johnson took the oath of office in the plane, and it departed.

Having been elected on his own merit, on January 20, 1965, the principals began the festivities by attending services conducted by Protestant, Catholic, and Jewish clergymen at the National City Christian Church—an unprecedented interfaith ceremony on an inauguration day. The excitement of the day's event was made tense by the realization that the tight security along the route Johnson had to travel was motivated by what had happened in Dallas.

Mrs. Johnson held the Bible as her husband took the oath of office, the first time that a First Lady played a key role in a presidential inauguration. Johnson's brief address was an eloquent defense of his program for social change, which he called "the Great Society," a wide-ranging remaking of the nation's life that he saw as the chief goal of his administration.

Lyndon Baines Johnson
Inaugural Address

Wednesday, January 20, 1965

My fellow countrymen, on this occasion, the oath I have taken before you and before God is not mine alone, but ours together. We are one nation and one people. Our fate as a nation and our future as a people rest not upon one citizen, but upon all citizens.

This is the majesty and the meaning of this moment.

For every generation, there is a destiny. For some, history decides. For this generation, the choice must be our own.

Even now, a rocket moves toward Mars.[1] It reminds us that the world will not be the same for our children, or even for ourselves in a short span of years. The next man to stand here will look out on a scene different from our own, because ours is a time of change—rapid and fantastic change bearing the secrets of nature, multiplying the nations, placing in uncertain hands new weapons for mastery and destruction, shaking old values, and uprooting old ways.

Our destiny in the midst of change will rest on

---

1. *Mariner 3*, launched November 28, 1964, was scheduled to fly past Mars July 14, 1965.

the unchanged character of our people, and on their faith.

The American Covenant

They came here—the exile and the stranger, brave but frightened—to find a place where a man could be his own man. They made a covenant with this land. Conceived in justice, written in liberty, bound in union, it was meant one day to inspire the hopes of all mankind; and it binds us still. If we keep its terms, we shall flourish.

Justice and Change

First, justice was the promise that all who made the journey would share in the fruits of the land.

In a land of great wealth, families must not live in hopeless poverty. In a land rich in harvest, children just must not go hungry. In a land of healing miracles, neighbors must not suffer and die unattended. In a great land of learning and scholars, young people must be taught to read and write.

For the more than thirty years that I have served this nation, I have believed that this injustice to our people, this waste of our resources, was our real enemy. For thirty years or more, with the resources I have had, I have vigilantly fought against it. I have learned, and I know, that it will not surrender easily.

But change has given us new weapons. Before this generation of Americans is finished, this enemy will not only retreat—it will be conquered.

Justice requires us to remember that when any citizen denies his fellow, saying, "His color is not mine," or "His beliefs are strange and different," in that moment he betrays America, though his forebears created this Nation.

LIBERTY AND CHANGE

Liberty was the second article of our covenant. It was self-government. It was our Bill of Rights. But it was more. America would be a place where each man could be proud to be himself: stretching his talents, rejoicing in his work, important in the life of his neighbors and his nation.

This has become more difficult in a world where change and growth seem to tower beyond the control and even the judgment of men. We must work to provide the knowledge and the surroundings which can enlarge the possibilities of every citizen.

The American covenant called on us to help show the way for the liberation of man. And that is today our goal. Thus, if as a nation there is much outside our control, as a people no stranger is outside our hope.

Change has brought new meaning to that old mission. We can never again stand aside, prideful in isolation. Terrific dangers and troubles that we once called "foreign" now constantly live among us. If American lives must end, and American treasure be spilled, in countries we barely know, that is the price that change has demanded of conviction and of our enduring covenant.

Think of our world as it looks from the rocket that is heading toward Mars. It is like a child's globe, hanging in space, the continents stuck to its side like colored maps. We are all fellow passengers on a dot of earth. And each of us, in the span of time, has really only a moment among our companions.

How incredible it is that in this fragile existence, we should hate and destroy one another. There are possibilities enough for all who will abandon mastery over others to pursue mastery over nature. There is world enough for all to seek their happiness in their own way.

Our nation's course is abundantly clear. We aspire to nothing that belongs to others. We seek no dominion over our fellow man, but man's dominion over tyranny and misery.

But more is required. Men want to be a part of a common enterprise—a cause greater than themselves. Each of us must find a way to advance the purpose of the Nation, thus finding new purpose for ourselves. Without this, we shall become a nation of strangers.

U.S. infantry patrol moves against Viet Cong, Dak To, South Vietnam, June 7, 1966.

UNION AND CHANGE

The third article was union. To those who were small and few against the wilderness, the success of liberty demanded the strength of union. Two centuries of change have made this true again.

No longer need capitalist and worker, farmer and clerk, city and countryside, struggle to divide our bounty. By working shoulder to shoulder, together we can increase the bounty of all. We have discovered that every child who learns, every man who finds work, every sick body that is made whole—like a candle added to an altar—brightens the hope of all the faithful.

So let us reject any among us who seek to reopen old wounds and to rekindle old hatreds. They stand in the way of a seeking nation.

Let us now join reason to faith and action to experience, to transform our unity of interest into a unity of purpose. For the hour and the day and the time are here to achieve progress without strife, to achieve change without hatred—not without difference of opinion, but without the deep and abiding divisions which scar the union for generations.

THE AMERICAN BELIEF

Under this covenant of justice, liberty, and union we have become a nation—prosperous, great, and mighty. And we have kept our freedom. But we have no promise from God that our greatness will endure. We have been allowed by Him to seek greatness with the sweat of our hands and the strength of our spirit.

I do not believe that the Great Society[2] is the ordered, changeless, and sterile battalion of the ants. It is the excitement of becoming—always becoming, trying, probing, falling, resting, and trying again—but always trying and always gaining.

In each generation, with toil and tears, we have had to earn our heritage again.

If we fail now, we shall have forgotten in abundance what we learned in hardship: that democracy rests on faith, that freedom asks more than it gives, and that the judgment of God is harshest on those who are most favored.

If we succeed, it will not be because of what we have, but it will be because of what we are; not because of what we own, but, rather because of what we believe.

For we are a nation of believers. Underneath the clamor of building and the rush of our day's pursuits, we are believers in justice and liberty and

---

2. Johnson's vision for the country encompassed a series of domestic initiatives that he articulated in a speech at the University of Michigan, Ann Arbor, May 22, 1964. The Great Society Program became his agenda to Congress in 1965.

union, and in our own Union. We believe that every man must someday be free. And we believe in ourselves.

Our enemies have always made the same mistake. In my lifetime—in depression and in war—they have awaited our defeat. Each time, from the secret places of the American heart, came forth the faith they could not see or that they could not even imagine. It brought us victory. And it will again.

For this is what America is all about. It is the uncrossed desert and the unclimbed ridge. It is the star that is not reached and the harvest sleeping in the unplowed ground. Is our world gone? We say "Farewell." Is a new world coming? We welcome it—and we will bend it to the hopes of man.

To these trusted public servants and to my family and those close friends of mine who have followed me down a long, winding road, and to all the people of this Union and the world, I will repeat today what I said on that sorrowful day in November 1963: "I will lead and I will do the best I can."[3]

But you must look within your own hearts to the old promises and to the old dream. They will lead you best of all.

---

3. President John F. Kennedy was assassinated in Dallas, Texas, November 22, 1963.

Demonstrators march on Michigan Avenue during the 1968 Democratic Convention in Chicago, Illinois.

For myself, I ask only, in the words of an ancient leader: "Give me now wisdom and knowledge, that I may go out and come in before this people: for who can judge this thy people, that is so great?"[4]

---

4. Chronicles 2:10.

Richard Milhous Nixon

37th President of the United States
1969–74

Richard Milhous Nixon

BORN: January 9, 1913, Yorba Linda, Calif.
MARRIED: Thelma Catherine "Pat" Ryan, June 21,
1940; two children
DIED: April 22, 1994, New York, N.Y.
PARTY: Republican
EDUCATION: Public schools; Whittier College (1934);
Duke University Law School (1937).

CAREER:
Lawyer in Calif.; attorney, Office of Emergency Management, Washington, D.C. (1942); U.S. Navy (1942–46);
U.S. House of Representatives (1947–51); U.S. Senate
(1951–53); vice president (1953–61); Republican candidate
for president (1960); lost bid for California governor (1962);
president (1969–74); resigned Aug. 9, 1974; pardoned by
Gerald R. Ford, Sept. 8, 1974; retired to New York.

PRESIDENTIAL CAMPAIGNS:
1960: With former Senator Henry Cabot Lodge Jr. of
Massachusetts lost to Kennedy and Johnson.
1968: Nixon and Maryland Governor Spiro T. Agnew
defeated Democratic Vice President Hubert H.
Humphrey and Senator Edmund S. Muskie of Maine.
1972: Scored the second-largest victory in history against
Senator George S. McGovern, a liberal South Dakota
Democrat who did not have the full support of his party.

Richard and Patricia Nixon at the Great Wall during his historic visit to China, February 1972.

Introduction

Richard Nixon's and John Kennedy's lives were destined to be linked. Both came to the House of Representatives in 1946. A vigorous conservative who developed a national following for his role in the investigation of the Soviet spy Alger Hiss, Nixon was named Eisenhower's running mate in 1952.

He became a national hero by debating Soviet Premier Nikita Khrushchev in the exhibit of an American kitchen in Moscow in 1959. Ironically, agreeing to debate his presidential opponent in 1960 proved a mistake. The public concluded that Nixon was not equal to Kennedy in substance or charisma.

Still, the election was the closest since 1888, with Kennedy winning by a mere 100,000 votes. Nixon believed that fraud was involved—but declined to press the issue. In 1962, after losing a bid to be governor of California, he told reporters: "You won't have Nixon to kick around anymore, because, gentlemen, this is my last press conference."

But he did return. In 1968, he seemed to represent Americans' hopes for more order and stability in the face of the anti–Vietnam War uprisings taking place throughout the country. And, he pledged to end the war.

In taking the oath of office, Nixon delivered a forceful speech that reflected some of the power of Kennedy's inaugural and also Lincoln's second.

Richard Milhous Nixon
First Inaugural Address

Monday, January 20, 1969

Senator Dirksen, Mr. Chief Justice, Mr. Vice President, President Johnson, Vice President Humphrey[1], my fellow Americans—and my fellow citizens of the world community:

I ask you to share with me today the majesty of this moment. In the orderly transfer of power, we celebrate the unity that keeps us free.

Each moment in history is a fleeting time, precious and unique. But some stand out as moments of beginning, in which courses are set that shape decades or centuries.

This can be such a moment.

Forces now are converging that make possible, for the first time, the hope that many of man's deepest aspirations can at last be realized. The spiraling pace of change allows us to contemplate, within our own lifetime, advances that once would have taken centuries.

In throwing wide the horizons of space, we have discovered new horizons on earth.

---

1. Senator Everett McKinley Dirksen (1896–1969) (R–IL), 1951–69; Earl Warren (1891–1974), chief justice of the United States, 1953–69; Spiro Theodore Agnew (1918–96), thirty-ninth vice president, 1969–73; President Lyndon Baines Johnson; Hubert Horatio Humphrey (1911–78), thirty-eighth vice president, 1965–69.

For the first time, because the people of the world want peace, and the leaders of the world are afraid of war, the times are on the side of peace.

Eight years from now America will celebrate its 200th anniversary as a nation. Within the lifetime of most people now living, mankind will celebrate that great new year which comes only once in a thousand years—the beginning of the third millennium.

What kind of nation we will be, what kind of world we will live in, whether we shape the future in the image of our hopes, is ours to determine by our actions and our choices.

The greatest honor history can bestow is the title of peacemaker. This honor now beckons America—the chance to help lead the world at last out of the valley of turmoil, and onto that high ground of peace that man has dreamed of since the dawn of civilization.

If we succeed, generations to come will say of us now living that we mastered our moment, that we helped make the world safe for mankind.

This is our summons to greatness.

I believe the American people are ready to answer this call.

The second third of this century has been a time of proud achievement. We have made enormous strides in science and industry and agriculture. We have shared our wealth more broadly than ever. We have learned at last to manage a modern economy to assure its continued growth.

We have given freedom new reach, and we have begun to make its promise real for black as well as for white.

We see the hope of tomorrow in the youth of today. I know America's youth. I believe in them. We can be proud that they are better educated, more committed, more passionately driven by conscience than any generation in our history.

No people has ever been so close to the achievement of a just and abundant society, or so possessed of the will to achieve it. Because our strengths are so great, we can afford to appraise our weaknesses with candor and to approach them with hope.

Standing in this same place a third of a century ago, Franklin Delano Roosevelt addressed a nation ravaged by depression and gripped in fear. He could say in surveying the nation's troubles: "They concern, thank God, only material things."

Our crisis today is the reverse.

We have found ourselves rich in goods, but ragged in spirit; reaching with magnificent precision for the moon, but falling into raucous discord on earth.

We are caught in war, wanting peace. We are torn by division, wanting unity. We see around us empty lives, wanting fulfillment. We see tasks that need doing, waiting for hands to do them.

To a crisis of the spirit, we need an answer of the spirit.

To find that answer, we need only look within ourselves.

When we listen to "the better angels of our nature,"[2] we find that they celebrate the simple things, the basic things—such as goodness, decency, love, kindness.

Greatness comes in simple trappings.

The simple things are the ones most needed today if we are to surmount what divides us, and cement what unites us.

To lower our voices would be a simple thing.

In these difficult years, America has suffered from a fever of words; from inflated rhetoric that promises more than it can deliver; from angry rhetoric that fans discontents into hatreds; from bombastic rhetoric that postures instead of persuading.

We cannot learn from one another until we stop shouting at one another—until we speak quietly enough so that our words can be heard as well as our voices.

For its part, government will listen. We will strive to listen in new ways—to the voices of quiet anguish, the voices that speak without words, the voices of the heart—to the injured voices, the anxious voices, the voices that have despaired of being heard.

---

2. A phrase from President Abraham Lincoln's first inaugural address, March 4, 1861.

Those who have been left out, we will try to bring in.

Those left behind, we will help to catch up.

For all of our people, we will set as our goal the decent order that makes progress possible and our lives secure.

As we reach toward our hopes, our task is to build on what has gone before—not turning away from the old, but turning toward the new.

In this past third of a century, government has passed more laws, spent more money, initiated more programs, than in all our previous history.

In pursuing our goals of full employment, better housing, excellence in education; in rebuilding our cities and improving our rural areas; in protecting our environment and enhancing the quality of life—in all these and more, we will and must press urgently forward.

We shall plan now for the day when our wealth can be transferred from the destruction of war abroad to the urgent needs of our people at home.

The American dream does not come to those who fall asleep.

But we are approaching the limits of what government alone can do.

Our greatest need now is to reach beyond government, and to enlist the legions of the concerned and the committed.

What has to be done, has to be done by government and people together or it will not be done at all. The lesson of past agony is that without the people we can do nothing; with the people we can do everything.

To match the magnitude of our tasks, we need the energies of our people—enlisted not only in grand enterprises, but more importantly in those small, splendid efforts that make headlines in the neighborhood newspaper instead of the national journal.

With these, we can build a great cathedral of the spirit—each of us raising it one stone at a time, as he reaches out to his neighbor, helping, caring, doing.

I do not offer a life of uninspiring ease. I do not call for a life of grim sacrifice. I ask you to join in a high adventure—one as rich as humanity itself, and as exciting as the times we live in.

The essence of freedom is that each of us shares in the shaping of his own destiny.

Until he has been part of a cause larger than himself, no man is truly whole.

The way to fulfillment is in the use of our talents; we achieve nobility in the spirit that inspires that use.

As we measure what can be done, we shall promise only what we know we can produce, but as we chart our goals we shall be lifted by our dreams.

No man can be fully free while his neighbor is not. To go forward at all is to go forward together.

This means black and white together, as one nation, not two. The laws have caught up with our conscience. What remains is to give life to what is in the law: to ensure at last that as all are born equal in dignity before God, all are born equal in dignity before man.

As we learn to go forward together at home, let us also seek to go forward together with all mankind.

Let us take as our goal: where peace is unknown, make it welcome; where peace is fragile, make it strong; where peace is temporary, make it permanent.

After a period of confrontation, we are entering an era of negotiation.

Let all nations know that during this administration our lines of communication will be open.

We seek an open world—open to ideas, open to the exchange of goods and people—a world in which no people, great or small, will live in angry isolation.

We cannot expect to make everyone our friend, but we can try to make no one our enemy.

Those who would be our adversaries, we invite to a peaceful competition—not in conquering territory or extending dominion, but in enriching the life of man.

As we explore the reaches of space, let us go to the new worlds together—not as new worlds to be conquered, but as a new adventure to be shared.

With those who are willing to join, let us cooperate to reduce the burden of arms, to strengthen the structure of peace, to lift up the poor and the hungry.

But to all those who would be tempted by weakness, let us leave no doubt that we will be as strong as we need to be for as long as we need to be.

Over the past twenty years, since I first came to this capital as a freshman congressman, I have visited most of the nations of the world.

I have come to know the leaders of the world, and the great forces, the hatreds, the fears that divide the world.

I know that peace does not come through wishing for it—that there is no substitute for days and even years of patient and prolonged diplomacy.

I also know the people of the world.

I have seen the hunger of a homeless child, the pain of a man wounded in battle, the grief of a mother who has lost her son. I know these have no ideology, no race.

I know America. I know the heart of America is good.

I speak from my own heart, and the heart of my country, the deep concern we have for those who suffer, and those who sorrow.

I have taken an oath today in the presence of God and my countrymen to uphold and defend the Constitution of the United States. To that oath I now add this sacred commitment: I shall consecrate my office, my energies, and all the wisdom I can summon, to the cause of peace among nations.

Let this message be heard by strong and weak alike:

The peace we seek to win is not victory over any other people, but the peace that comes "with healing in its wings";[3] with compassion for those who have suffered; with understanding for those who have opposed us; with the opportunity for all the peoples of this earth to choose their own destiny.

Only a few short weeks ago, we shared the glory of man's first sight of the world as God sees it, as a single sphere reflecting light in the darkness.

As the Apollo astronauts flew over the moon's gray surface on Christmas Eve,[4] they spoke to us of the beauty of earth—and in that voice so clear across the lunar distance, we heard them invoke God's blessing on its goodness.

In that moment, their view from the moon moved poet Archibald MacLeish to write:

"To see the earth as it truly is, small and blue and beautiful in that eternal silence where it floats, is to see ourselves as riders on the earth together, brothers on that bright loveliness in the eternal cold—brothers who know now they are truly brothers."[5]

---

3. Malachi 4:2.

4. Apollo 8 mission: December 21–27, 1968, was the first manned spacecraft to leave earth's gravity and reach the moon.

5. From an essay by Archibald MacLeish (1892–1982), American poet, scholar, and ninth librarian of Congress, published on the front page of the *New York Times,* December 25, 1968.

"That's one small step for a man . . . and one giant leap for mankind." U.S. astronauts plant the American flag on the moon, July 20, 1969.

In that moment of surpassing technological triumph, men turned their thoughts toward home and humanity—seeing in that far perspective that man's destiny on earth is not divisible; telling us that however far we reach into the cosmos, our destiny lies not in the stars but on Earth itself, in our own hands, in our own hearts.

We have endured a long night of the American spirit. But as our eyes catch the dimness of the first rays of dawn, let us not curse the remaining dark. Let us gather the light.

Our destiny offers, not the cup of despair, but the chalice of opportunity. So let us seize it, not in fear, but in gladness—and, "riders on the earth together," let us go forward, firm in our faith, steadfast in our purpose, cautious of the dangers; but sustained by our confidence in the will of God and the promise of man.

Introduction

Richard Nixon's second campaign seemed from the start a sure victory. The people were impressed by the skill and imaginativeness of his administration in opening relations with The People's Republic of China and improving those with the Soviet Union.

The election soon became complicated. George McGovern and the Democrats denounced Nixon for "dirty tricks" and directed attention to a White House–inspired break-in at the Democratic headquarters in Washington's Watergate complex. The affair led to an attempt by the administration to conceal its participation in this crime. Nixon was not personally involved in the burglary, but he was heavily implicated in its cover-up. A great struggle ensued to make public Nixon's tapes of White House conversations to learn what they revealed about Watergate. Once the Supreme Court ordered the tapes to be surrendered, Nixon was doomed.

Nevertheless, Nixon delivered a stirring inaugural, outlining the role the United States would play in bringing peace among nations. We do not know whether as he spoke he was privately agonized by what Watergate might do to his hopes and dreams. Only a few days before his second term began, the first Watergate trial started. Step after step thereafter led Nixon down-hill, ending in August 1974 in his resignation before he could be impeached and removed from the presidency. He is the only chief executive to leave office in disgrace.

Richard Milhous Nixon
Second Inaugural Address

Saturday, January 20, 1973

Mr. Vice President, Mr. Speaker, Mr. Chief Justice, Senator Cook, Mrs. Eisenhower,[1] and my fellow citizens of this great and good country we share together:

When we met here four years ago, America was bleak in spirit, depressed by the prospect of seemingly endless war abroad and of destructive conflict at home.

As we meet here today, we stand on the threshold of a new era of peace in the world.

The central question before us is: How shall we use that peace? Let us resolve that this era we are about to enter will not be what other postwar periods have so often been: a time of retreat and isolation that leads to stagnation at home and invites new danger abroad.

Let us resolve that this will be what it can become: a time of great responsibilities greatly

---

1. Spiro Theodore Agnew (1918–96), thirty-ninth vice president, 1969–73; John William McCormack (1891–1980) (D–MA), congressman, 1928–71, Speaker of the House of Representatives, 1961–71; Earl Warren (1891–1974), chief justice of the United States, 1953–69; Marlow Webster Cook (1926–) (R–KY), senator, 1967–74; Mamie Doud Eisenhower (1896–1979), widow of President Dwight Eisenhower.

borne, in which we renew the spirit and the promise of America as we enter our third century as a nation.

This past year saw far-reaching results from our new policies for peace. By continuing to revitalize our traditional friendships, and by our missions to Peking and to Moscow, we were able to establish the base for a new and more durable pattern of relationships among the nations of the world.

Because of America's bold initiatives, 1972 will be long remembered as the year of the greatest progress since the end of World War II toward a lasting peace in the world.

The peace we seek in the world is not the flimsy peace which is merely an interlude between wars, but a peace which can endure for generations to come.

It is important that we understand both the necessity and the limitations of America's role in maintaining that peace.

Unless we in America work to preserve the peace, there will be no peace.

Unless we in America work to preserve freedom, there will be no freedom.

But let us clearly understand the new nature of America's role, as a result of the new policies we have adopted over these past four years.

We shall respect our treaty commitments.

We shall support vigorously the principle that no country has the right to impose its will or rule on another by force.

We shall continue, in this era of negotiation, to work for the limitation of nuclear arms, and to reduce the danger of confrontation between the great powers.

We shall do our share in defending peace and freedom in the world. But we shall expect others to do their share.

The time has passed when America will make every other nation's conflict our own, or make every other nation's future our responsibility, or presume to tell the people of other nations how to manage their own affairs.

Just as we respect the right of each nation to determine its own future, we also recognize the responsibility of each nation to secure its own future.

Just as America's role is indispensable in preserving the world's peace, so is each nation's role indispensable in preserving its own peace.

Together with the rest of the world, let us resolve to move forward from the beginnings we have made. Let us continue to bring down the walls of hostility which have divided the world for too long, and to build in their place bridges of understanding—so that despite profound differences between systems of government, the people of the world can be friends.

Let us build a structure of peace in the world in which the weak are as safe as the strong—in which each respects the right of the other to live by a dif-

ferent system—in which those who would influence others will do so by the strength of their ideas,
and not by the force of their arms.

Let us accept that high responsibility not as a
burden, but gladly—gladly because the chance to
build such a peace is the noblest endeavor in which
a nation can engage; gladly, also, because only if we
act greatly in meeting our responsibilities abroad
will we remain a great nation, and only if we remain
a great nation will we act greatly in meeting our
challenges at home.

We have the chance today to do more than ever
before in our history to make life better in America—
to ensure better education, better health, better housing, better transportation, a cleaner environment—to
restore respect for law, to make our communities
more livable—and to insure the God-given right of
every American to full and equal opportunity.

Because the range of our needs is so great—
because the reach of our opportunities is so great—
let us be bold in our determination to meet those
needs in new ways.

Just as building a structure of peace abroad has
required turning away from old policies that failed,
so building a new era of progress at home requires
turning away from old policies that have failed.

Abroad, the shift from old policies to new has
not been a retreat from our responsibilities, but a
better way to peace.

Surrounded by family, President Nixon says goodbye in the East Room of the White House after his resignation, August 9, 1974.

And at home, the shift from old policies to new will not be a retreat from our responsibilities, but a better way to progress.

Abroad and at home, the key to those new responsibilities lies in the placing and the division of responsibility. We have lived too long with the consequences of attempting to gather all power and responsibility in Washington.

Abroad and at home, the time has come to turn away from the condescending policies of paternalism—of "Washington knows best."

A person can be expected to act responsibly only if he has responsibility. This is human nature. So let us encourage individuals at home and nations abroad to do more for themselves, to decide more for themselves. Let us locate responsibility in more places. Let us measure what we will do for others by what they will do for themselves.

That is why today I offer no promise of a purely governmental solution for every problem. We have lived too long with that false promise. In trusting too much in government, we have asked of it more than it can deliver. This leads only to inflated expectations, to reduced individual effort, and to a disappointment and frustration that erode confidence both in what government can do and in what people can do.

Government must learn to take less from people so that people can do more for themselves.

Let us remember that America was built not by government, but by people—not by welfare, but by work—not by shirking responsibility, but by seeking responsibility.

In our own lives, let each of us ask—not just what will government do for me, but what can I do for myself?

In the challenges we face together, let each of us ask—not just how can government help, but how can I help?

Your national government has a great and vital role to play. And I pledge to you that where this Government should act, we will act boldly and we will lead boldly. But just as important is the role that each and every one of us must play, as an individual and as a member of his own community.

From this day forward, let each of us make a solemn commitment in his own heart: to bear his responsibility, to do his part, to live his ideals—so that together, we can see the dawn of a new age of progress for America, and together, as we celebrate our 200th anniversary as a nation, we can do so proud in the fulfillment of our promise to ourselves and to the world.

As America's longest and most difficult war comes to an end, let us again learn to debate our differences with civility and decency. And let each of us reach out for that one precious quality government cannot provide—a new level of respect for the rights and feelings of one another, a new level of respect for the individual human dignity which is the cherished birthright of every American.

Above all else, the time has come for us to renew our faith in ourselves and in America.

In recent years, that faith has been challenged.

Our children have been taught to be ashamed of their country, ashamed of their parents, ashamed of America's record at home and of its role in the world.

At every turn, we have been beset by those who find everything wrong with America and little that is right. But I am confident that this will not be the judgment of history on these remarkable times in which we are privileged to live.

America's record in this century has been unparalleled in the world's history for its responsibility, for its generosity, for its creativity and for its progress.

Let us be proud that our system has produced and provided more freedom and more abundance, more widely shared, than any other system in the history of the world.

Let us be proud that in each of the four wars in which we have been engaged in this century, including the one we are now bringing to an end, we have fought not for our selfish advantage, but to help others resist aggression.

Let us be proud that by our bold, new initiatives, and by our steadfastness for peace with honor, we have made a breakthrough toward creating in the world what the world has not known before—a structure of peace that can last, not merely for our time, but for generations to come.

We are embarking here today on an era that presents challenges great as those any nation, or any generation, has ever faced.

We shall answer to God, to history, and to our conscience for the way in which we use these years.

As I stand in this place, so hallowed by history, I think of others who have stood here before me. I think of the dreams they had for America, and I think of how each recognized that he needed help far beyond himself in order to make those dreams come true.

Today, I ask your prayers that in the years ahead I may have God's help in making decisions that are right for America, and I pray for your help so that together we may be worthy of our challenge.

Let us pledge together to make these next four years the best four years in America's history, so that on its 200th birthday America will be as young and as vital as when it began, and as bright a beacon of hope for all the world.

Let us go forward from here confident in hope, strong in our faith in one another, sustained by our faith in God who created us, and striving always to serve His purpose.

Gerald Rudolph Ford Jr.

38th President of the United States
1974–77

Gerald Rudolph Ford Jr.

BORN: July 14, 1913, Omaha, Neb. (as Leslie Lynch King Jr.; took name of mother's second husband)
MARRIED: Elizabeth Bloomer "Betty" Warren, October 15, 1948; four children
PARTY: Republican
EDUCATION: South High School, Grand Rapids, Mich.; University of Michigan (1935); Yale University Law School (1941).

CAREER:
Lawyer in Grand Rapids; U.S. Navy (1942–46); U.S. House of Representatives (1949–73); minority leader (1965–1973); appointed vice president (under the provisions of the Twenty-fifth Amendment) December 6, 1973; vice president (1973–74); president (1974–77); retired to Rancho Mirage, Calif.

PRESIDENTIAL CAMPAIGNS:
1973: Became president upon Nixon's resignation, August 9, 1974. An early act—widely criticized—was to grant Nixon a full pardon.
1976: Running with Kansas Senator Robert Dole, he was defeated in a comparatively close canvass by the Democratic governor of Georgia, Jimmy Carter. Ford had damaged his chances by performing poorly in the presidential debates.

Gerald Ford takes the oath of office at the White House administered by Chief Justice Warren Burger as Betty Ford looks on, August 9, 1974.

A U.S. helicopter evacuates Vietnamese refugees as Saigon falls, April 29, 1975.

James Earl Carter Jr.
39th President of the United States
1977–81

James Earl "Jimmy" Carter Jr.

BORN: October 1, 1924, Plains, Ga.
MARRIED: Eleanor Rosalynn Smith, July 7, 1946;
four children
PARTY: Democratic
EDUCATION: Public schools; Georgia Southwestern
College (1941–42); Georgia Institute of Technology
(1942–43); U.S. Naval Academy (1946).

CAREER:
U.S. Navy officer (1946–53); resigned to take over family peanut farm and supply business; Georgia Senate
(1963–66); ran for governor in 1966 and lost; governor
of Georgia (1971–75); president (1977–81); returned to
Georgia to write books, teach university, and volunteer;
became international leader in conflict resolution;
Nobel Peace Prize (2002).

PRESIDENTIAL CAMPAIGN:
1976: Traded on his lack of experience in Washington
politics by soothing the public's post-Watergate distrust
of government with his promise: "I will never tell a lie
to the American people." Intensely campaigning for a
year, he and running mate Senator Walter Mondale of
Minnesota captured 41,000,000 votes to President
Ford's 39,000,000.

*Egyptian President Sadat, U.S. President Carter and
Israeli Prime Minister Begin clasp hands at the Camp David
Accords signing ceremony, September 17, 1978.*

INTRODUCTION

J immy Carter's election as president had an extraordinary history. Nixon's departure had made Vice
President Gerald R. Ford Jr. the new president. Ford
was minority leader in the House of Representatives
when Congress, pursuant to the Twenty-fifth Amendment, named him vice president (1973) following
Spiro T. Agnew's forced resignation after pleading no
contest to criminal charges of tax evasion. Ford, in
turn, selected New York Governor Nelson A. Rocke-
feller as his vice president. The nation thus had both of
its highest political offices occupied by men not elected
to them. The Democrats, feeling they could not lose in
1976, confidently selected a relative unknown, Georgia
Governor Jimmy Carter.

Carter was the first president from the Deep South
since Zachary Taylor in 1849. He took the oath of
office on two Bibles: one a gift from his mother, the
other the same used by George Washington at his
swearing-in. The inaugural address was short, taking
only seventeen minutes to deliver. The early quotation
from Micah may have been a subtle approval of Ford's
full pardon of Nixon from legal action.

Carter, his wife, Rosalynn, and their nine-year-old
daughter, Amy—in an unprecedented act—walked
together the mile and a half back from the Capitol to
the White House rather than riding in a limousine.

James Earl Carter, Jr.
Inaugural Address

Thursday, January 20, 1977

For myself and for our nation, I want to thank my predecessor[1] for all he has done to heal our land.

In this outward and physical ceremony we attest once again to the inner and spiritual strength of our nation. As my high school teacher, Miss Julia Coleman, used to say: "We must adjust to changing times and still hold to unchanging principles."

Here before me is the Bible used in the inauguration of our first president, in 1789, and I have just taken the oath of office on the Bible my mother gave me a few years ago, opened to a timeless admonition from the ancient prophet Micah:

"He hath showed thee, O man, what is good; and what doth the Lord require of thee, but to do justly, and to love mercy, and to walk humbly with thy God."[2]

This inauguration ceremony marks a new beginning, a new dedication within our government, and a new spirit among us all. A president may sense

---

1. President Gerald Ford (1913–), fortieth vice president, 1974–77—first selected under process of Twenty-fifth Amendment; thirty-eighth president. Ford succeeded to the presidency following Nixon's resignation in 1974.
2 Micah 6:8.

and proclaim that new spirit, but only a people can provide it.

Two centuries ago our nation's birth was a milestone in the long quest for freedom, but the bold and brilliant dream which excited the founders of this nation still awaits its consummation. I have no new dream to set forth today, but rather urge a fresh faith in the old dream.

Ours was the first society openly to define itself in terms of both spirituality and of human liberty. It is that unique self-definition which has given us an exceptional appeal, but it also imposes on us a special obligation, to take on those moral duties which, when assumed, seem invariably to be in our own best interests.

You have given me a great responsibility—to stay close to you, to be worthy of you, and to exemplify what you are. Let us create together a new national spirit of unity and trust. Your strength can compensate for my weakness, and your wisdom can help to minimize my mistakes.

Let us learn together and laugh together and work together and pray together, confident that in the end we will triumph together in the right.

The American dream endures. We must once again have full faith in our country—and in one another. I believe America can be better. We can be even stronger than before.

Let our recent mistakes bring a resurgent com-

Jimmy and Rosalynn Carter walk from the Capitol to the White House after his inauguration, January 20, 1977.

mitment to the basic principles of our Nation, for we know that if we despise our own government we have no future. We recall in special times when we have stood briefly, but magnificently, united. In those times no prize was beyond our grasp.

But we cannot dwell upon remembered glory. We cannot afford to drift. We reject the prospect of failure or mediocrity or an inferior quality of life for any person. Our government must at the same time be both competent and compassionate.

We have already found a high degree of personal liberty, and we are now struggling to enhance equality of opportunity. Our commitment to human rights must be absolute, our laws fair, our natural beauty preserved; the powerful must not persecute the weak, and human dignity must be enhanced.

We have learned that "more" is not necessarily "better," that even our great nation has its recognized limits, and that we can neither answer all questions nor solve all problems. We cannot afford to do everything, nor can we afford to lack boldness as we meet the future. So, together, in a spirit of individual sacrifice for the common good, we must simply do our best.

Our nation can be strong abroad only if it is strong at home. And we know that the best way to enhance freedom in other lands is to demonstrate here that our democratic system is worthy of emulation.

To be true to ourselves, we must be true to others. We will not behave in foreign places so as to violate our rules and standards here at home, for we know that the trust which our nation earns is essential to our strength.

The world itself is now dominated by a new spirit. Peoples more numerous and more politically aware are craving and now demanding their place in the sun—not just for the benefit of their own physical condition, but for basic human rights.

The passion for freedom is on the rise. Tapping this new spirit, there can be no nobler nor more ambitious task for America to undertake on this day of a new beginning than to help shape a just and peaceful world that is truly humane.

We are a strong nation, and we will maintain strength so sufficient that it need not be proven in combat—a quiet strength based not merely on the size of an arsenal, but on the nobility of ideas.

We will be ever vigilant and never vulnerable, and we will fight our wars against poverty, ignorance, and injustice—for those are the enemies against which our forces can be honorably marshaled.

We are a purely idealistic nation, but let no one confuse our idealism with weakness.

Because we are free we can never be indifferent to the fate of freedom elsewhere. Our moral sense dictates a clear-cut preference for these societies which share with us an abiding respect for individual human rights. We do not seek to intimidate, but it is clear that a world which others can dominate with impunity would be inhospitable to decency and a threat to the well-being of all people.

The world is still engaged in a massive armaments race designed to ensure continuing equivalent strength among potential adversaries. We pledge perseverance and wisdom in our efforts to limit the world's armaments to those necessary for each nation's own domestic safety. And we will move this year a step toward ultimate goal—the elimination of all nuclear weapons from this Earth. We urge all other people to join us, for success can mean life instead of death.

Within us, the people of the United States, there is evident a serious and purposeful rekindling of confidence. And I join in the hope that when my time as your president has ended, people might say this about our Nation:

—that we had remembered the words of Micah and renewed our search for humility, mercy, and justice;

—that we had torn down the barriers that separated those of different race and region and religion, and where there had been mistrust, built unity, with a respect for diversity;

—that we had found productive work for those able to perform it;

—that we had strengthened the American family, which is the basis of our society;

—that we had ensured respect for the law, and equal treatment under the law, for the weak and the powerful, for the rich and the poor;

—and that we had enabled our people to be proud of their own government once again.

I would hope that the nations of the world might say that we had built a lasting peace, built not on weapons of war but on international policies which reflect our own most precious values.

These are not just my goals, and they will not be my accomplishments, but the affirmation of our Nation's continuing moral strength and our belief in an undiminished, ever-expanding American dream.

Ronald Wilson Reagan

40th President of the United States
1981–89

Ronald Wilson Reagan

BORN: February 6, 1911, Tampico, Ill.
MARRIED: Jane Wyman, Jan. 25, 1940; two children;
divorced 1948. Nancy Davis, March 4, 1952; two children
DIED: June 5, 2004, Los Angeles, Calif.
PARTY: Republican
EDUCATION: Public schools; Eureka College (1932).

CAREER:
Radio announcer (1932–37); motion picture and television actor (1937–65); U.S. Army (1942–45); president,
Screen Actors Guild (1947–52; 1959–60); California
governor (1967–75); businessman, rancher, commenta-
tor on public policy (1975–80); unsuccessful bid for
president (1976); president (1981–89); retired to Calif.

PRESIDENTIAL CAMPAIGNS:
1980: With George H.W. Bush as vice president, Reagan won by 8,500,000 votes over incumbent Carter;
Independent Congressman John B. Anderson of Illinois
had made it a three-way race. Reagan became the oldest
president and the first who had been divorced.
1984: Challenged by Democratic Senator Walter Mondale of Minnesota and New York Congresswoman
Geraldine Ferraro, the first woman nominated for vice
president. Reagan took every state except Mondale's
Minnesota and the District of Columbia.

*President Reagan and Soviet General Secretary Gorbachev
in Red Square, Moscow, the Soviet Union, May 31, 1988.*

Introduction

Ronald Reagan's face was known to millions from his movies, but the public only gradually learned his political views. Initially a Democrat, over time he became a social and fiscal conservative, positions avidly backed by his wife, Nancy, a true political partner. His speech at the 1964 Republican convention supporting Barry Goldwater motivated Republicans to draft him for California governor.

Reagan's presidential campaign was aided by the Iranian hostage crisis that Carter couldn't end. The American embassy staff had been held prisoner since November 4, 1979, as a protest against America's recent support of the Shah. Reagan's experience in front of microphones made him a master in debates with Carter. He especially scored with the question: "Are you better off than you were four years ago?"

The inauguration was moved to the West Front of the Capitol, a tribute to Reagan's love of the American West. His address was brief—only twenty minutes— and recycled many of his campaign speeches. He spoke of "national renewal," aware that anger over Watergate and the Vietnam War persisted, and promised to reduce taxes and hold government spending. Just as he was finishing, the Iranian government released the 52 American hostages and sent them home. No administration had ever begun on such a happy turn of events.

Ronald Wilson Reagan
First Inaugural Address

Tuesday, January 20, 1981

Senator Hatfield, Mr. Chief Justice, Mr. President, Vice President Bush, Vice President Mondale, Senator Baker, Speaker O'Neill, Reverend Moomaw,[1] and my fellow citizens: To a few of us here today, this is a solemn and most momentous occasion; and yet, in the history of our nation, it is a commonplace occurrence. The orderly transfer of authority as called for in the Constitution routinely takes place as it has for almost two centuries and few of us stop to think how unique we really are. In the eyes of many in the world, this every-four-year ceremony we accept as normal is nothing less than a miracle.

Mr. President, I want our fellow citizens to know how much you did to carry on this tradition. By your gracious cooperation in the transition process, you have shown a watching world that we are a

---

1. Mark Odom Hatfield (1922–   ) (R–OR), senator, 1967–97; Warren Earl Burger (1907–95), chief justice of the United States, 1969–86; President James Earl Carter Jr.; George Herbert Walker Bush (1924–   ), forty-third vice president, 1981–89; Walter Frederick Mondale (1928–   ), forty-second vice president, 1977–81; Howard Henry Baker Jr. (1925–   ) (R–TN), senator, 1966–85; Thomas Phillip "Tip" O'Neill Jr. (1912–94) (D–MA), congressman, 1953–87, Speaker of the House of Representatives, 1981–87; Rev. Donn Moomaw, Bel Air Presbyterian Church, Los Angeles.

President Reagan greets freed Iran hostages and their families at the White House, January 27, 1981.

united people pledged to maintaining a political system which guarantees individual liberty to a greater degree than any other, and I thank you and your people for all your help in maintaining the continuity which is the bulwark of our republic.

The business of our nation goes forward. These United States are confronted with an economic affliction of great proportions. We suffer from the longest and one of the worst sustained inflations in our national history. It distorts our economic decisions, penalizes thrift, and crushes the struggling young and the fixed-income elderly alike. It threatens to shatter the lives of millions of our people.

Idle industries have cast workers into unemployment, causing human misery and personal indignity. Those who do work are denied a fair return for their labor by a tax system which penalizes successful achievement and keeps us from maintaining full productivity.

But great as our tax burden is, it has not kept pace with public spending. For decades, we have piled deficit upon deficit, mortgaging our future and our children's future for the temporary convenience of the present. To continue this long trend is to guarantee tremendous social, cultural, political, and economic upheavals.

You and I, as individuals, can, by borrowing, live beyond our means, but for only a limited period of time. Why, then, should we think that collectively, as a nation, we are not bound by that same limitation?

We must act today in order to preserve tomorrow. And let there be no misunderstanding—we are going to begin to act, beginning today.

The economic ills we suffer have come upon us over several decades. They will not go away in days, weeks, or months, but they will go away. They will go away because we, as Americans, have the capacity now, as we have had in the past, to do whatever needs to be done to preserve this last and greatest bastion of freedom.

In this present crisis, government is not the solution to our problem.

From time to time, we have been tempted to believe that society has become too complex to be managed by self-rule, that government by an elite group is superior to government for, by, and of the people. But if no one among us is capable of governing himself, then who among us has the capacity to govern someone else? All of us together, in and out of government, must bear the burden. The solutions we seek must be equitable, with no one group singled out to pay a higher price.

We hear much of special interest groups. Our concern must be for a special interest group that has been too long neglected. It knows no sectional boundaries or ethnic and racial divisions, and it crosses political party lines. It is made up of men and women who raise our food, patrol our streets, man our mines and our factories, teach our children, keep our homes, and heal us when we are sick—professionals, industrialists, shopkeepers, clerks, cabbies, and truckdrivers. They are, in short, "We the people," this breed called Americans.

Well, this administration's objective will be a healthy, vigorous, growing economy that provides equal opportunity for all Americans, with no barriers born of bigotry or discrimination. Putting America back to work means putting all Americans back to work. Ending inflation means freeing all Americans from the terror of runaway living costs. All must share in the productive work of this "new beginning" and all must share in the bounty of a revived economy. With the idealism and fair play which are the core of our system and our strength, we can have a strong and prosperous America at peace with itself and the world.

So, as we begin, let us take inventory. We are a nation that has a government—not the other way around. And this makes us special among the nations of the Earth. Our government has no power except that granted it by the people. It is time to check and reverse the growth of government which shows signs of having grown beyond the consent of the governed.

It is my intention to curb the size and influence of the federal establishment and to demand recognition of the distinction between the powers granted to the federal government and those reserved to the states or to the people. All of us need to be reminded that the federal government did not create the states; the states created the federal government.

Now, so there will be no misunderstanding, it is not my intention to do away with government. It is, rather, to make it work—work with us, not over us; to stand by our side, not ride on our back. Government can and must provide opportunity, not smother it; foster productivity, not stifle it.

If we look to the answer as to why, for so many years, we achieved so much, prospered as no other people on Earth, it was because here, in this land, we unleashed the energy and individual genius of man to a greater extent than has ever been done before. Freedom and the dignity of the individual have been more available and assured here than in any other place on Earth. The price for this freedom at times has been high, but we have never been unwilling to pay that price.

It is no coincidence that our present troubles parallel and are proportionate to the intervention and intrusion in our lives that result from unnecessary and excessive growth of government. It is time for us to realize that we are too great a nation to limit ourselves to small dreams. We are not, as some would have us believe, doomed to an inevitable decline. I do not believe in a fate that will fall on us no matter what we do. I do believe in a fate that will fall on us if we do nothing. So, with all the creative energy at our command, let us begin an era of national renewal. Let us renew our determination, our courage, and our strength. And let us renew our faith and our hope.

We have every right to dream heroic dreams. Those who say that we are in a time when there are no heroes just don't know where to look. You can see heroes every day going in and out of factory gates. Others, a handful in number, produce enough food to feed all of us and then the world beyond. You meet heroes across a counter—and they are on both sides of that counter. There are entrepreneurs with faith in themselves and faith in an idea, who create new jobs, new wealth and opportunity. They are individuals and families whose taxes support the government and whose voluntary gifts support church, charity, culture, art, and education. Their patriotism is quiet but deep. Their values sustain our national life.

I have used the words "they" and "their" in speaking of these heroes. I could say "you" and "your" because I am addressing the heroes of whom I speak—you, the citizens of this blessed land. Your dreams, your hopes, your goals are going to be the dreams, the hopes, and the goals of this administration, so help me God.

We shall reflect the compassion that is so much a

part of your makeup. How can we love our country and not love our countrymen, and loving them, reach out a hand when they fall, heal them when they are sick, and provide opportunities to make them self-sufficient so they will be equal in fact and not just in theory?

Can we solve the problems confronting us? Well, the answer is an unequivocal and emphatic "yes." To paraphrase Winston Churchill, I did not take the oath I have just taken with the intention of presiding over the dissolution of the world's strongest economy.[2]

In the days ahead I will propose removing the roadblocks that have slowed our economy and reduced productivity. Steps will be taken aimed at restoring the balance between the various levels of government. Progress may be slow—measured in inches and feet, not miles—but we will progress. Is it time to reawaken this industrial giant, to get government back within its means, and to lighten our punitive tax burden. And these will be our first priorities, and on these principles, there will be no compromise.

On the eve of our struggle for independence a man who might have been one of the greatest among

---

2. "I have not become the King's First Minister in order to preside over the liquidation of the British Empire." Winston Churchill, prime minister, Great Britain, speech, Mansion House, London, November 10, 1942.

the Founding Fathers, Dr. Joseph Warren,[3] president of the Massachusetts Congress, said to his fellow Americans, "Our country is in danger, but not to be despaired of . . . . On you depend the fortunes of America. You are to decide the important questions upon which rests the happiness and the liberty of millions yet unborn. Act worthy of yourselves."

Well, I believe we, the Americans of today, are ready to act worthy of ourselves, ready to do what must be done to ensure happiness and liberty for ourselves, our children, and our children's children.

And as we renew ourselves here in our own land, we will be seen as having greater strength throughout the world. We will again be the exemplar of freedom and a beacon of hope for those who do not now have freedom.

To those neighbors and allies who share our freedom, we will strengthen our historic ties and assure them of our support and firm commitment. We will match loyalty with loyalty. We will strive for mutually beneficial relations. We will not use our friendship to impose on their sovereignty, for our own sovereignty is not for sale.

As for the enemies of freedom, those who are potential adversaries, they will be reminded that peace is the highest aspiration of the American peo-

---

3. Dr. Joseph Warren (1741–75), Revolutionary War patriot killed at the battle of Bunker Hill, Boston, Massachusetts, June 17, 1775.

After the assassination attempt on President Reagan, James Brady and police officer Thomas Delahanty lie wounded outside the Washington Hilton Hotel, March 30, 1981.

ple. We will negotiate for it, sacrifice for it; we will not surrender for it—now or ever.

Our forbearance should never be misunderstood. Our reluctance for conflict should not be misjudged as a failure of will. When action is required to preserve our national security, we will act. We will maintain sufficient strength to prevail if need be, knowing that if we do so we have the best chance of never having to use that strength.

Above all, we must realize that no arsenal, or no weapon in the arsenals of the world, is so formidable as the will and moral courage of free men and women. It is a weapon our adversaries in today's world do not have. It is a weapon that we as Americans do have. Let that be understood by those who practice terrorism and prey upon their neighbors.

I am told that tens of thousands of prayer meetings are being held on this day, and for that I am deeply grateful. We are a nation under God, and I believe God intended for us to be free. It would be fitting and good, I think, if on each Inauguration Day in future years it should be declared a day of prayer.

This is the first time in history that this ceremony has been held, as you have been told, on this West Front of the Capitol. Standing here, one faces a magnificent vista, opening up on this city's special beauty and history. At the end of this open mall are those shrines to the giants on whose shoulders we stand.

Directly in front of me, the monument to a monumental man: George Washington, Father of our Country. A man of humility who came to greatness reluctantly. He led America out of revolutionary victory into infant nationhood. Off to one side, the stately memorial to Thomas Jefferson. The Declaration of Independence flames with his eloquence.

And then beyond the Reflecting Pool the dignified columns of the Lincoln Memorial. Whoever would understand in his heart the meaning of America will find it in the life of Abraham Lincoln.

Beyond those monuments to heroism is the Potomac River, and on the far shore the sloping hills of Arlington National Cemetery with its row on row of simple white markers bearing crosses or Stars of David. They add up to only a tiny fraction of the price that has been paid for our freedom.

Each one of those markers is a monument to the kinds of hero I spoke of earlier. Their lives ended in places called Belleau Wood, The Argonne, Omaha Beach, Salerno, and halfway around the world on Guadalcanal, Tarawa, Pork Chop Hill, the Chosin Reservoir, and in a hundred rice paddies and jungles of a place called Vietnam.

Under one such marker lies a young man—Martin Treptow—who left his job in a small town barber shop in 1917 to go to France with the famed Rainbow Division. There, on the western front, he was killed trying to carry a message between battalions under heavy artillery fire.

We are told that on his body was found a diary. On the flyleaf under the heading, "My Pledge," he had written these words: "America must win this war. Therefore, I will work, I will save, I will sacrifice, I will endure, I will fight cheerfully and do my utmost, as if the issue of the whole struggle depended on me alone."

The crisis we are facing today does not require of us the kind of sacrifice that Martin Treptow and so many thousands of others were called upon to make. It does require, however, our best effort, and our willingness to believe in ourselves and to believe in our capacity to perform great deeds; to believe that together, with God's help, we can and will resolve the problems which now confront us.

And, after all, why shouldn't we believe that? We are Americans. God bless you, and thank you.

INTRODUCTION

Ronald Reagan ran for reelection with widespread public approval. His phrases had thrilled audiences throughout the country: America was a "shining city upon a hill"; the Soviet Union was "an evil empire"; citizens had the right to "dream heroic dreams." His sunny personality enabled him to deflect criticism, earning him the nickname "the Teflon president." His personal courage was also recognized. After being severely wounded in an attempted assassination in March 1981, his first public words were warm and even witty.

His 1984 campaign opponent, Walter Mondale, hurt himself by saying that he would raise taxes. Reagan was slowing up, and his responses in their debates were less effective than four years earlier. Still, he quipped warmly when accused by Mondale of being too old for the presidency: "I'm not going to exploit for political purposes my opponent's youth and inexperience."

Reagan was sworn in on Sunday, January 20, in the grand foyer of the White House. On Monday, Reagan took the oath of office again in the rotunda of the Capitol. An outdoor ceremony was out of the question because the temperature had fallen to −2 °F, and, for the first time since Andrew Jackson's time, the inauguration parade had to be canceled. The inaugural address, taking only eighteen minutes, was a call for a new assault on barriers to free enterprise.

Ronald Wilson Reagan
Second Inaugural Address

Monday, January 21, 1985

Senator Mathias, Chief Justice Burger, Vice President Bush, Speaker O'Neill, Senator Dole,[1] Reverend Clergy, members of my family and friends, and my fellow citizens:

This day has been made brighter with the presence here of one who, for a time, has been absent—Senator John Stennis.[2]

God bless you and welcome back.

There is, however, one who is not with us today: Representative Gillis Long[3] of Louisiana left us last night. I wonder if we could all join in a moment of silent prayer. *[Moment of silent prayer.]* Amen.

There are no words adequate to express my thanks for the great honor that you have bestowed on me. I will do my utmost to be deserving of your trust.

---

1. Senator Charles McCurdy Mathias, Jr. (1922–   ) (R–MD), 1969–87; Warren Earl Burger (1909–95), chief justice of the United States, 1969–86; George Herbert Walker Bush (1924–   ), forty-third vice president; Thomas Phillip "Tip" O'Neill Jr. (1912–94) (D–MA), congressman, 1953–87, Speaker of the House of Representatives, 1981–87; Senator Robert Joseph Dole (1923–   ) (R–KS), 1969–96.
2. Senator John Cornelius Stennis (1901–95) (D–MS), 1947–89; recovered from a recent illness to attend the inauguration.
3. Gillis William Long (1923–85) (D–LA), congressman, 1963–64, 1973–85; died January 20, 1985.

This is, as Senator Mathias told us, the fiftieth time that we the people have celebrated this historic occasion. When the first president, George Washington, placed his hand upon the Bible, he stood less than a single day's journey by horseback from raw, untamed wilderness. There were four million Americans in a union of thirteen states. Today we are sixty times as many in a union of fifty states. We have lighted the world with our inventions, gone to the aid of mankind wherever in the world there was a cry for help, journeyed to the Moon and safely returned. So much has changed. And yet we stand together as we did two centuries ago.

When I took this oath four years ago, I did so in a time of economic stress. Voices were raised saying we had to look to our past for the greatness and glory. But we, the present-day Americans, are not given to looking backward. In this blessed land, there is always a better tomorrow.

Four years ago, I spoke to you of a new beginning and we have accomplished that. But in another sense, our new beginning is a continuation of that beginning created two centuries ago when, for the first time in history, government, the people said, was not our master, it is our servant; its only power that which we the people allow it to have.

That system has never failed us, but, for a time, we failed the system. We asked things of government that government was not equipped to give. We yielded authority to the national government that properly belonged to states or to local governments or to the people themselves. We allowed taxes and inflation to rob us of our earnings and savings and watched the great industrial machine that had made us the most productive people on Earth slow down and the number of unemployed increase.

By 1980, we knew it was time to renew our faith, to strive with all our strength toward the ultimate in individual freedom consistent with an orderly society.

We believed then and now there are no limits to growth and human progress when men and women are free to follow their dreams.

And we were right to believe that. Tax rates have been reduced, inflation cut dramatically, and more people are employed than ever before in our history.

We are creating a nation once again vibrant, robust, and alive. But there are many mountains yet to climb. We will not rest until every American enjoys the fullness of freedom, dignity, and opportunity as our birthright. It is our birthright as citizens of this great Republic, and we'll meet this challenge.

These will be years when Americans have restored their confidence and tradition of progress; when our values of faith, family, work, and neighborhood were restated for a modern age; when our economy was finally freed from government's grip; when we made sincere efforts at meaningful arms reduction, rebuilding our defenses, our economy, and developing new technologies, and helped preserve peace in a troubled world; when Americans courageously supported the struggle for liberty, self-government, and free enterprise throughout the world, and turned the tide of history away from totalitarian darkness and into the warm sunlight of human freedom.

My fellow citizens, our Nation is poised for greatness. We must do what we know is right and do it with all our might. Let history say of us, "These were golden years—when the American Revolution was reborn, when freedom gained new life, when America reached for her best."

Our two-party system has served us well over the years, but never better than in those times of great challenge when we came together not as Democrats or Republicans, but as Americans united in a common cause.

Two of our Founding Fathers, a Boston lawyer named Adams and a Virginia planter named Jefferson, members of that remarkable group who met in Independence Hall and dared to think they could start the world over again, left us an important lesson. They had become political rivals in the presidential election of 1800. Then years later, when both were retired, and age had softened their anger, they began to speak to each other again through letters. A bond was reestablished between those two who had helped create this government of ours.

In 1826, the fiftieth anniversary of the Declaration of Independence, they both died. They died on the same day, within a few hours of each other, and that day was the Fourth of July.

In one of those letters exchanged in the sunset of their lives, Jefferson wrote: "It carries me back to the times when, beset with difficulties and dangers, we were fellow laborers in the same cause, struggling for what is most valuable to man, his right to self-government. Laboring always at the same oar, with some wave ever ahead threatening to overwhelm us, and yet passing harmless . . . we rode through the storm with heart and hand."

Well, with heart and hand, let us stand as one today: One people under God determined that our future shall be worthy of our past. As we do, we must not repeat the well-intentioned errors of our past. We must never again abuse the trust of working men and women, by sending their earnings on a futile chase after the spiraling demands of a bloated federal establishment. You elected us in 1980 to end this prescription for disaster, and I don't believe you reelected us in 1984 to reverse course.

At the heart of our efforts is one idea vindicated by twenty-five straight months of economic growth: Freedom and incentives unleash the drive and entrepreneurial genius that are the core of human progress. We have begun to increase the rewards for work, savings, and investment; reduce the increase in the cost and size of government and its interference in people's lives.

We must simplify our tax system, make it more fair, and bring the rates down for all who work and earn. We must think anew and move with a new boldness, so every American who seeks work can find work; so the least among us shall have an equal chance to achieve the greatest things—to be heroes who heal our sick, feed the hungry, protect peace among nations, and leave this world a better place.

The time has come for a new American emancipation—a great national drive to tear down economic barriers and liberate the spirit of enterprise in the most distressed areas of our country. My friends, together we can do this, and do it we must, so help me God. From new freedom will spring new opportunities for growth, a more productive, fulfilled, and united people, and a stronger America—an America that will lead the technological revolution, and also open its mind and heart and soul to the treasures of literature, music, and poetry, and the values of faith, courage, and love.

A dynamic economy, with more citizens working and paying taxes, will be our strongest tool to bring down budget deficits. But an almost unbroken fifty years of deficit spending has finally brought us to a time of reckoning. We have come to a turning point, a moment for hard decisions. I have asked the cabinet and my staff a question, and now I put the same question to all of you: If not us, who? And if not now, when? It must be done by all of us going forward with a program aimed at reaching a balanced budget. We can then begin reducing the national debt.

I will shortly submit a budget to the Congress aimed at freezing government program spending for the next year. Beyond that, we must take further steps to permanently control government's power to tax and spend. We must act now to protect future generations from government's desire to spend its citizens' money and tax them into servitude when the bills come due. Let us make it unconstitutional for the federal government to spend more than the federal government takes in.

We have already started returning to the people and to state and local governments responsibilities better handled by them.

Now, there is a place for the federal government in matters of social compassion. But our fundamental goals must be to reduce dependency and upgrade the dignity of those who are infirm or disadvantaged. And here a growing economy and support from family and community offer our best chance for a society where compassion is a way of life, where the old and infirm are cared for, the young and, yes, the unborn protected, and the unfortunate looked after and made self-sufficient.

And there is another area where the federal government can play a part. As an older American, I remember a time when people of different race, creed, or ethnic origin in our land found hatred and prejudice installed in social custom and, yes, in law. There is no story more heartening in our history than the progress that we have made toward the "brotherhood of man" that God intended for us. Let us resolve there will be no turning back or hesitation on the road to an America rich in dignity and abundant with opportunity for all our citizens.

Let us resolve that we the people will build an American opportunity society in which all of us—white and black, rich and poor, young and old—will go forward together arm in arm. Again, let us remember that though our heritage is one of blood lines from every corner of the Earth, we are all Americans pledged to carry on this last, best hope of man on Earth.

I have spoken of our domestic goals and the limitations which we should put on our national government. Now let me turn to a task which is the primary responsibility of national government—the safety and security of our people.

Today, we utter no prayer more fervently than the ancient prayer for peace on Earth. Yet history has shown that peace will not come, nor will our freedom be preserved, by good will alone. There are those in the world who scorn our vision of human dignity and freedom. One nation, the Soviet Union, has conducted the greatest military buildup in the history of man, building arsenals of awesome offensive weapons.

We have made progress in restoring our defense capability. But much remains to be done. There must be no wavering by us, nor any doubts by others, that America will meet her responsibilities to remain free, secure, and at peace.

There is only one way safely and legitimately to reduce the cost of national security, and that is to reduce the need for it. And this we are trying to do in negotiations with the Soviet Union. We are not just discussing limits on a further increase of nuclear weapons. We seek, instead, to reduce their number. We seek the total elimination one day of nuclear weapons from the face of the Earth.

Now, for decades, we and the Soviets have lived under the threat of mutual assured destruction; if either resorted to the use of nuclear weapons, the other could retaliate and destroy the one who had started it. Is there either logic or morality in believing that if one side threatens to kill tens of millions of our people, our only recourse is to threaten killing tens of millions of theirs?

I have approved a research program to find, if we can, a security shield that would destroy nuclear missiles before they reach their target. It wouldn't kill people, it would destroy weapons. It wouldn't militarize space, it would help demilitarize the arsenals of Earth. It would render nuclear weapons obsolete. We will meet with the Soviets, hoping that we can agree on a way to rid the world of the threat of nuclear destruction.

We strive for peace and security, heartened by the changes all around us. Since the turn of the century, the number of democracies in the world has grown fourfold. Human freedom is on the march, and nowhere more so than our own hemisphere. Freedom is one of the deepest and noblest aspirations of the human spirit. People, worldwide, hunger for the right of self-determination, for those inalienable rights that make for human dignity and progress.

America must remain freedom's staunchest friend, for freedom is our best ally.

And it is the world's only hope, to conquer poverty and preserve peace. Every blow we inflict against poverty will be a blow against its dark allies of oppression and war. Every victory for human freedom will be a victory for world peace.

So we go forward today, a nation still mighty in its youth and powerful in its purpose. With our alliances strengthened, with our economy leading the world to a new age of economic expansion, we look forward to a world rich in possibilities. And all this because we have worked and acted

Extreme cold weather in Washington, D.C., forces President Reagan's second inauguration inside the Capitol rotunda, Washington, D.C., January 21, 1985.

together, not as members of political parties, but as Americans.

My friends, we live in a world that is lit by lightning. So much is changing and will change, but so much endures, and transcends time.

History is a ribbon, always unfurling; history is a journey. And as we continue our journey, we think of those who traveled before us. We stand together again at the steps of this symbol of our democracy—or we would have been standing at the steps if it hadn't gotten so cold. Now we are standing inside this symbol of our democracy. Now we hear again the echoes of our past: a general falls to his knees in the hard snow of Valley Forge; a lonely president paces the darkened halls, and ponders his struggle to preserve the Union; the men of the Alamo call out encouragement to each other; a settler pushes west and sings a song, and the song echoes out forever and fills the unknowing air.

It is the American sound. It is hopeful, bighearted, idealistic, daring, decent, and fair. That's our heritage; that is our song. We sing it still. For all our problems, our differences, we are together as of old, as we raise our voices to the God who is the Author of this most tender music. And may He continue to hold us close as we fill the world with our sound—sound in unity, affection, and love— one people under God, dedicated to the dream of freedom that He has placed in the human heart, called upon now to pass that dream on to a waiting and hopeful world.

God bless you and may God bless America.

George Herbert Walker Bush

41st President of the United States
1989–93

George Herbert Walker Bush

BORN: June 12, 1924, Milton, Mass.
MARRIED: Barbara Pierce, Jan. 6, 1945; six children
PARTY: Republican
EDUCATION: Phillips Academy (1942); Yale University
(1948).

CAREER:
U.S. Navy pilot (Distinguished Flying Cross), World
War II; oil industry executive; U.S. congressman from
Texas (1967–71); various government posts in 1970s,
including ambassador to the United Nations, chief of
U.S. Liaison Office in China, CIA director; vice presi-
dent (1981–89); president (1989–93); retired to Houston.

PRESIDENTIAL CAMPAIGNS:
1988: Ran with forty-one-year-old Indiana Senator J.
Danforth "Dan" Quayle to magnetize votes of younger
citizens. Defeated Massachusetts Governor Michael
Dukakis and Senator Lloyd Bentsen of Texas. Dukakis,
after starting with an early lead, ran a poor campaign.
1992: Defeated by charismatic Arkansas Governor Bill
Clinton, who made Bush appear old-fashioned and
unconnected to changes in American society.

President George H.W. and Barbara Bush attend an inaugural ball, January 20, 1989.

INTRODUCTION

George Bush was the first vice president to succeed to the presidency without the death of the incumbent president since Martin Van Buren followed Andrew Jackson into the White House in 1837.

Having faithfully served Reagan, Bush had won the respect of Republican leaders and gained the nomination. Bush is remembered for comments made during his campaign. He offered his high hope for a "kinder, gentler America," and promised that he would not support a rise in taxes. To emphasize his promise he boldly added his assurance, "Read my lips!" Those words, which had been inserted by his speechwriter, would prove to be a wicked barrier to reelection because Bush later had to support a tax increase.

Bush, a hero pilot in the navy during World War II, drew on the public's appreciation of his heroism by using a photograph of his crashed plane.

The people were attracted by Bush's low-key style, noting that he wore a simple business suit for his oath-taking. Still, the festivities connected with his inauguration were the most expensive in history. He took the oath of office from Chief Justice William Rehnquist, and in his brief inaugural—lasting twenty minutes—he repeated his hope for a kinder America. And, not being a scrapper, he said he looked forward to bipartisanship, which, he recalled, had once characterized the relations between presidents and Congress.

George Herbert Walker Bush
Inaugural Address

Friday, January 20, 1989

Mr. Chief Justice, Mr. President, Vice President Quayle, Senator Mitchell, Speaker Wright, Senator Dole, Congressman Michel,[1] and fellow citizens, neighbors, and friends:

There is a man here who has earned a lasting place in our hearts and in our history. President Reagan, on behalf of our Nation, I thank you for the wonderful things that you have done for America.

I have just repeated word for word the oath taken by George Washington 200 years ago, and the Bible on which I placed my hand is the Bible on which he placed his.[2] It is right that the memory of Washington be with us today, not only because this

---

1. William Hubbs Rehnquist (1924–2005), chief justice of the United States, 1986– ; President Ronald Wilson Reagan; James Danforth Quayle III (1947–), forty-fourth vice president, 1989–93; George John Mitchell (1933–) (D–ME), senator, 1979–94; Congressman James Claude Wright Jr. (1922–) (D–TX), Speaker of the House of Representatives, 1987–90; Senator Robert Joseph Dole (1923–) (R–KS), 1969–96; Congressman Robert Henry Michel (1923–) (R–IL) 1957–94.
2. Washington's inaugural Bible was also used by Warren Harding, Dwight Eisenhower, and Jimmy Carter. This King James Bible, printed in London in 1767, is owned by the St. John's Lodge No. 1, Ancient York Masons, Free & Accepted Masons, the oldest Lodge in New York State.

is our Bicentennial Inauguration, but because Washington remains the Father of our Country. And he would, I think, be gladdened by this day; for today is the concrete expression of a stunning fact: our continuity these 200 years since our government began.

We meet on democracy's front porch, a good place to talk as neighbors and as friends. For this is a day when our nation is made whole, when our differences, for a moment, are suspended.

And my first act as president is a prayer. I ask you to bow your heads:

Heavenly Father, we bow our heads and thank You for Your love. Accept our thanks for the peace that yields this day and the shared faith that makes its continuance likely. Make us strong to do Your work, willing to heed and hear Your will, and write on our hearts these words: "Use power to help people." For we are given power not to advance our own purposes, nor to make a great show in the world, nor a name. There is but one just use of power, and it is to serve people. Help us to remember it, Lord. Amen.

I come before you and assume the presidency at a moment rich with promise. We live in a peaceful, prosperous time, but we can make it better. For a new breeze is blowing, and a world refreshed by freedom seems reborn; for in man's heart, if not in fact, the day of the dictator is over. The totalitarian era is passing, its old ideas blown away like leaves from an ancient, lifeless tree. A new breeze is blowing, and a nation refreshed by freedom stands ready to push on. There is new ground to be broken, and new action to be taken. There are times when the future seems thick as a fog; you sit and wait, hoping the mists will lift and reveal the right path. But this is a time when the future seems a door you can walk right through into a room called tomorrow.

Great nations of the world are moving toward democracy through the door to freedom. Men and women of the world move toward free markets through the door to prosperity. The people of the world agitate for free expression and free thought through the door to the moral and intellectual satisfactions that only liberty allows.

We know what works: Freedom works. We know what's right: Freedom is right. We know how to secure a more just and prosperous life for man on Earth: through free markets, free speech, free elections, and the exercise of free will unhampered by the state.

For the first time in this century, for the first time in perhaps all history, man does not have to invent a system by which to live. We don't have to talk late into the night about which form of government is better. We don't have to wrest justice from the kings. We only have to summon it from within ourselves. We must act on what we know. I take as my guide

The Berlin Wall, long a symbol of the cold war, is pulled down at the Brandenburg Gate, November 11, 1989.

the hope of a saint: In crucial things, unity; in important things, diversity; in all things, generosity.[3]

America today is a proud, free nation, decent and civil, a place we cannot help but love. We know in our hearts, not loudly and proudly, but as a simple fact, that this country has meaning beyond what we see, and that our strength is a force for good. But have we changed as a nation even in our time? Are we enthralled with material things, less appreciative of the nobility of work and sacrifice?

My friends, we are not the sum of our possessions. They are not the measure of our lives. In our hearts we know what matters. We cannot hope only to leave our children a bigger car, a bigger bank account. We must hope to give them a sense of what it means to be a loyal friend, a loving parent, a citizen who leaves his home, his neighborhood and town better than he found it. What do we want the men and women who work with us to say when we are no longer there? That we were more driven to succeed than anyone around us? Or that we stopped to ask if a sick child had gotten better, and stayed a moment there to trade a word of friendship?

No president, no government, can teach us to remember what is best in what we are. But if the

---

3. Paraphrase of "in necessary things, unity; in doubtful things, liberty; in all things, charity." Sometimes ascribed to St. Augustine (354–430), but also to Richard Baxter, English author and Puritan (1615–91).

man you have chosen to lead this government can help make a difference; if he can celebrate the quieter, deeper successes that are made not of gold and silk, but of better hearts and finer souls; if he can do these things, then he must.

America is never wholly herself unless she is engaged in high moral principle. We as a people have such a purpose today. It is to make kinder the face of the nation and gentler the face of the world. My friends, we have work to do. There are the homeless, lost and roaming. There are the children who have nothing, no love, no normalcy. There are those who cannot free themselves of enslavement to whatever addiction—drugs, welfare, the demoralization that rules the slums. There is crime to be conquered, the rough crime of the streets. There are young women to be helped who are about to become mothers of children they can't care for and might not love. They need our care, our guidance, and our education, though we bless them for choosing life.

The old solution, the old way, was to think that public money alone could end these problems. But we have learned that is not so. And in any case, our funds are low. We have a deficit to bring down. We have more will than wallet; but will is what we need. We will make the hard choices, looking at what we have and perhaps allocating it differently, making our decisions based on honest need and prudent safety. And then we will do the wisest thing of all: We will turn to the only resource we have that in times of need always grows—the goodness and the courage of the American people.

I am speaking of a new engagement in the lives of others, a new activism, hands-on and involved, that gets the job done. We must bring in the generations, harnessing the unused talent of the elderly and the unfocused energy of the young. For not only leadership is passed from generation to generation, but so is stewardship. And the generation born after the Second World War has come of age.

I have spoken of a thousand points of light, of all the community organizations that are spread like stars throughout the nation, doing good. We will work hand in hand, encouraging, sometimes leading, sometimes being led, rewarding. We will work on this in the White House, in the cabinet agencies. I will go to the people and the programs that are the brighter points of light, and I will ask every member of my government to become involved. The old ideas are new again because they are not old, they are timeless: duty, sacrifice, commitment, and a patriotism that finds its expression in taking part and pitching in.

We need a new engagement, too, between the Executive and the Congress. The challenges before us will be thrashed out with the House and the Senate. We must bring the federal budget into balance.

And we must ensure that America stands before the world united, strong, at peace, and fiscally sound. But, of course, things may be difficult. We need compromise; we have had dissension. We need harmony; we have had a chorus of discordant voices.

For Congress, too, has changed in our time. There has grown a certain divisiveness. We have seen the hard looks and heard the statements in which not each other's ideas are challenged, but each other's motives. And our great parties have too often been far apart and untrusting of each other. It has been this way since Vietnam. That war cleaves us still. But, friends, that war began in earnest a quarter of a century ago; and surely the statute of limitations has been reached. This is a fact: The final lesson of Vietnam is that no great nation can long afford to be sundered by a memory. A new breeze is blowing, and the old bipartisanship must be made new again.

To my friends—and yes, I do mean friends—in the loyal opposition—and yes, I mean loyal: I put out my hand. I am putting out my hand to you, Mr. Speaker. I am putting out my hand to you Mr. Majority Leader.[4] For this is the thing: This is the age of the offered hand. We can't turn back clocks,

---

4. Mr. Speaker is James Claude Wright, Speaker of the House of Representatives; Mr. Majority Leader is Senator George John Mitchell, Democratic leader of the Senate.

and I don't want to. But when our fathers were young, Mr. Speaker, our differences ended at the water's edge. And we don't wish to turn back time, but when our mothers were young, Mr. Majority Leader, the Congress and the Executive were capable of working together to produce a budget on which this nation could live. Let us negotiate soon and hard. But in the end, let us produce. The American people await action. They didn't send us here to bicker. They ask us to rise above the merely partisan. "In crucial things, unity"—and this, my friends, is crucial.

To the world, too, we offer new engagement and a renewed vow: We will stay strong to protect the peace. The "offered hand" is a reluctant fist; but once made, strong, and can be used with great effect. There are today Americans who are held against their will in foreign lands, and Americans who are unaccounted for. Assistance can be shown here, and will be long remembered. Good will begets good will. Good faith can be a spiral that endlessly moves on.

Great nations like great men must keep their word. When America says something, America means it, whether a treaty or an agreement or a vow made on marble steps. We will always try to speak clearly, for candor is a compliment, but subtlety, too, is good and has its place. While keeping our alliances and friendships around the world strong,

President George H. W. Bush eats Thanksgiving dinner with troops in Saudi Arabia during Operation Desert Storm, November 22, 1990.

ever strong, we will continue the new closeness with the Soviet Union, consistent both with our security and with progress. One might say that our new relationship in part reflects the triumph of hope and strength over experience. But hope is good, and so are strength and vigilance.

Here today are tens of thousands of our citizens who feel the understandable satisfaction of those who have taken part in democracy and seen their hopes fulfilled. But my thoughts have been turning the past few days to those who would be watching at home, to an older fellow who will throw a salute by himself when the flag goes by, and the women who will tell her sons the words of the battle hymns. I don't mean this to be sentimental. I mean that on days like this, we remember that we are all part of a continuum, inescapably connected by the ties that bind.

Our children are watching in schools throughout our great land. And to them I say, thank you for watching democracy's big day. For democracy belongs to us all, and freedom is like a beautiful kite that can go higher and higher with the breeze. And to all I say: No matter what your circumstances or where you are, you are part of this day, you are part of the life of our great nation.

A president is neither prince nor pope, and I don't seek a window on men's souls. In fact, I yearn for a greater tolerance, an easy-goingness about each other's attitudes and way of life.

There are few clear areas in which we as a society must rise up united and express our intolerance. The most obvious now is drugs. And when that first cocaine was smuggled in on a ship, it may as well have been a deadly bacteria, so much has it hurt the body, the soul of our country. And there is much to be done and to be said, but take my word for it: This scourge will stop.

And so, there is much to do; and tomorrow the work begins. I do not mistrust the future; I do not fear what is ahead. For our problems are large, but our heart is larger. Our challenges are great, but our will is greater. And if our flaws are endless, God's love is truly boundless.

Some see leadership as high drama, and the sound of trumpets calling, and sometimes it is that. But I see history as a book with many pages, and each day we fill a page with acts of hopefulness and meaning. The new breeze blows, a page turns, the story unfolds. And so today a chapter begins, a small and stately story of unity, diversity, and generosity—shared, and written, together.

Thank you. God bless you and God bless the United States of America.

William Jefferson Clinton

42nd President of the United States
1993–2001

William Jefferson "Bill" Clinton

BORN: Aug. 19, 1946, Hot Springs, Ark. (as William Jefferson Blythe IV; took surname of mother's second husband)
MARRIED: Hillary Rodham, Oct. 11, 1975; one child
PARTY: Democratic
EDUCATION: Public and Catholic schools; Georgetown University (1968); Rhodes scholar at Oxford University (1968–70); Yale Law School (1973).

CAREER:
Professor of Law, University of Arkansas (1973–76); Arkansas attorney general (1977–79); Arkansas governor (1979–81; 1983–92); law practice (1981–82); president (1993–2001); retired to New York.

PRESIDENTIAL CAMPAIGNS:
1992: Competed against incumbent Bush and Reform Party candidate Texas businessman H. Ross Perot. Clinton and vice presidential candidate, Tennessee Senator Albert Gore, campaigned with their wives on an unprecedented bus tour. They won handily with 45 million votes—the largest number for Democrats ever. Perot, taking 19 percent, hurt Bush more than Clinton.
1996: In another three-way race, Clinton and Gore overwhelmed Republican Senator Robert Dole of Kansas and Perot. For the second time they won by a plurality, not a majority.

*President Clinton plays the saxophone at an inaugural ball,
January 20, 1993.*

Introduction

B ill Clinton had long hoped to be president. In 1992, his gift for fundraising and a charisma that was ideal on television gave him an edge over President George H. W. Bush, who had been riding high in the middle years of his administration but lacked campaign energy. One associate described Bush as a "reluctant warrior."

Three elements seemed to hinder Clinton: his alleged marital infidelity, his admitted use of marijuana earlier in his life (although he said he did not inhale), and his avoiding the draft during the Vietnam War. He overcame these much-discussed drawbacks through formidable public performances in the media and town meetings. Clinton became known as the "Comeback Kid" after he finished second in the New Hampshire primary and then developed his foothold nationally.

Another skillful marketing tool was the film, "The Man from Hope," shown at the Democratic convention in New York City. It presented Clinton as a young man who triumphed over poverty, thus offering hope to others who started at the bottom of life's heap.

Clinton's inaugural address, one of the shortest in history, took only fourteen minutes to deliver. It contained a tribute to Bush, his predecessor—an unusual step for an incoming president, especially one from another party—and made an appeal for Americans to reestablish their unity and self-confidence.

William Jefferson Clinton
First Inaugural Address

Wednesday, January 20, 1993

My fellow citizens:

Today we celebrate the mystery of American renewal.

This ceremony is held in the depth of winter. But, by the words we speak and the faces we show the world, we force the spring. A spring reborn in the world's oldest democracy, that brings forth the vision and courage to reinvent America.

When our founders boldly declared America's independence to the world and our purposes to the Almighty, they knew that America, to endure, would have to change. Not change for change's sake, but change to preserve America's ideals; life, liberty, the pursuit of happiness. Though we march to the music of our time, our mission is timeless. Each generation of Americans must define what it means to be an American.

On behalf of our Nation, I salute my predecessor, President Bush, for his half-century of service to America. And I thank the millions of men and women whose steadfastness and sacrifice triumphed over depression, fascism, and communism.

Today, a generation raised in the shadows of the cold war assumes new responsibilities in a world warmed by the sunshine of freedom but threatened still by ancient hatreds and new plagues.

Raised in unrivaled prosperity, we inherit an economy that is still the world's strongest, but is weakened by business failures, stagnant wages, increasing inequality, and deep divisions among our people.

When George Washington first took the oath I have just sworn to uphold, news traveled slowly across the land by horseback and across the ocean by boat. Now, the sights and sounds of this ceremony are broadcast instantaneously to billions around the world.

Communications and commerce are global; investment is mobile; technology is almost magical; and ambition for a better life is now universal. We earn our livelihood in peaceful competition with people all across the earth.

Profound and powerful forces are shaking and remaking our world, and the urgent question of our time is whether we can make change our friend and not our enemy.

This new world has already enriched the lives of millions of Americans who are able to compete and win in it. But when most people are working harder for less; when others cannot work at all; when the cost of health care devastates families and threatens to bankrupt many of our enterprises, great and small; when fear of crime robs law-abiding citizens of their freedom; and when millions of poor children cannot even imagine the lives we are calling them to lead, we have not made change our friend.

We know we have to face hard truths and take strong steps. But we have not done so. Instead, we have drifted, and that drifting has eroded our resources, fractured our economy, and shaken our confidence.

Though our challenges are fearsome, so are our strengths. And Americans have ever been a restless, questing, hopeful people. We must bring to our task today the vision and will of those who came before us.

From our revolution, the Civil War, to the Great Depression to the civil rights movement, our people have always mustered the determination to construct from these crises the pillars of our history.

Thomas Jefferson believed that to preserve the very foundations of our Nation, we would need dramatic change from time to time. Well, my fellow citizens, this is our time. Let us embrace it.

Our democracy must be not only the envy of the world but the engine of our own renewal. There is nothing wrong with America that cannot be cured by what is right with America.

And so today, we pledge an end to the era of deadlock and drift; a new season of American renewal has begun. To renew America, we must be bold. We must do what no generation has had to do before. We must invest more in our own people, in their jobs, in their future, and at the same time cut our massive debt. And we must do so in a world in which we must compete for every opportunity. It will not be easy; it will require sacrifice. But it can be done, and done fairly, not choosing sacrifice for its own sake, but for our own sake.

We must provide for our nation the way a family provides for its children. Our Founders saw themselves in the light of posterity. We can do no less. Anyone who has ever watched a child's eyes wander into sleep knows what posterity is. Posterity is the world to come; the world for whom we hold our ideals, from whom we have borrowed our planet, and to whom we bear sacred responsibility. We must do what America does best: offer more opportunity to all and demand responsibility from all.

It is time to break the bad habit of expecting something for nothing, from our government or from each other. Let us all take more responsibility, not only for ourselves and our families but for our communities and our country. To renew America, we must revitalize our democracy.

This beautiful capital, like every capital since the dawn of civilization, is often a place of intrigue and calculation. Powerful people maneuver for position and worry endlessly about who is in and who is out, who is up and who is down, forgetting those people whose toil and sweat sends us here and pays our way.

Americans deserve better, and in this city today,

there are people who want to do better. And so I say to all of us here, let us resolve to reform our politics, so that power and privilege no longer shout down the voice of the people. Let us put aside personal advantage so that we can feel the pain and see the promise of America. Let us resolve to make our government a place for what Franklin Roosevelt called "bold, persistent experimentation," a government for our tomorrows, not our yesterdays. Let us give this capital back to the people to whom it belongs.

To renew America, we must meet challenges abroad as well at home. There is no longer division between what is foreign and what is domestic—the world economy, the world environment, the world AIDS crisis, the world arms race—they affect us all.

Today, as an old order passes, the new world is more free but less stable. Communism's collapse has called forth old animosities and new dangers. Clearly America must continue to lead the world we did so much to make.

While America rebuilds at home, we will not shrink from the challenges, nor fail to seize the opportunities, of this new world. Together with our friends and allies, we will work to shape change, lest it engulf us.

When our vital interests are challenged, or the will and conscience of the international community is defied, we will act; with peaceful diplomacy when ever possible, with force when necessary. The brave

Americans serving our nation today in the Persian Gulf, in Somalia, and wherever else they stand are testament to our resolve.

But our greatest strength is the power of our ideas, which are still new in many lands. Across the world, we see them embraced, and we rejoice. Our hopes, our hearts, our hands, are with those on every continent who are building democracy and freedom. Their cause is America's cause.

The American people have summoned the change we celebrate today. You have raised your voices in an unmistakable chorus. You have cast your votes in historic numbers. And you have changed the face of Congress, the presidency and the political process itself. Yes, you, my fellow Americans have forced the spring. Now, we must do the work the season demands.

To that work I now turn, with all the authority of my office. I ask the Congress to join with me. But no president, no Congress, no government, can undertake this mission alone. My fellow Americans, you, too, must play your part in our renewal. I challenge a new generation of young Americans to a season of service; to act on your idealism by helping troubled children, keeping company with those in need, reconnecting our torn communities. There is so much to be done; enough indeed for millions of others who are still young in spirit to give of themselves in service, too.

In serving, we recognize a simple but powerful truth, we need each other. And we must care for one another. Today, we do more than celebrate America; we rededicate ourselves to the very idea of America.

An idea born in revolution and renewed through two centuries of challenge. An idea tempered by the knowledge that, but for fate we, the fortunate and the unfortunate, might have been each other. An idea ennobled by the faith that our Nation can summon from its myriad diversity the deepest measure of unity. An idea infused with the conviction that America's long heroic journey must go forever upward.

And so, my fellow Americans, at the edge of the twenty-first century, let us begin with energy and hope, with faith and discipline, and let us work until our work is done. The scripture says, "And let us not be weary in well-doing, for in due season, we shall reap, if we faint not."[1]

From this joyful mountaintop of celebration, we hear a call to service in the valley. We have heard the trumpets. We have changed the guard. And now, each in our way, and with God's help, we must answer the call.

Thank you, and God bless you all.

---

1. Galatians 6:9.

Introduction

Clinton's first term was not an outstanding success. He asked Hillary Rodham Clinton, the First Lady, to revolutionize health insurance; her efforts did not succeed. His foreign policy seemed uninspired: A humanitarian military mission to Somalia proved bloody; military involvement in the Balkans brought no political advantage.

But the Comeback Kid began to see that the old "New Deal" spirit had died. He slowly moved toward the political center, eager to balance the national budget and provide tax relief for the middle class. The changes proposed by Republican Speaker of the House Newt Gingrich of Georgia failed, and Republican efforts to shut down the government to force Clinton to accept their budget backfired.

The 1996 presidential campaign was made to order for Clinton, lacking as it did real issues. Senator Robert Dole, at seventy-three, was no match for the young, vigorous, and revived Clinton, who said in his acceptance speech: "The real choice is whether we build a bridge to the future or to the past." Dole called Clinton a liberal, but Clinton was now a conservative, no longer speaking of what he would do for the poor or other special groups.

In his inaugural, Clinton focused on the new century about to begin and he referred to the Internet—a first in inaugural speeches—as a sign of the changes coming to America.

William Jefferson Clinton
Second Inaugural Address

Monday, January 20, 1997

My fellow citizens:

At this last presidential inauguration of the twentieth century, let us lift our eyes toward the challenges that await us in the next century. It is our great good fortune that time and chance have put us not only at the edge of a new century, in a new millennium, but on the edge of a bright new prospect in human affairs, a moment that will define our course, and our character, for decades to come. We must keep our old democracy forever young. Guided by the ancient vision of a promised land, let us set our sights upon a land of new promise.

The promise of America was born in the eighteenth century out of the bold conviction that we are all created equal. It was extended and preserved in the nineteenth century, when our Nation spread across the continent, saved the Union, and abolished the awful scourge of slavery.

Then, in turmoil and triumph, that promise exploded onto the world stage to make this the American Century.

And what a century it has been. America became the world's mightiest industrial power; saved the world from tyranny in two world wars and a long

347

cold war; and time and again, reached out across the globe to millions who, like us, longed for the blessings of liberty.

Along the way, Americans produced a great middle class and security in old age; built unrivaled centers of learning and opened public schools to all; split the atom and explored the heavens; invented the computer and the microchip; and deepened the wellspring of justice by making a revolution in civil rights for African Americans and all minorities, and extending the circle of citizenship, opportunity, and dignity to women.

Now, for the third time, a new century is upon us, and another time to choose. We began the nineteenth century with a choice, to spread our Nation from coast to coast. We began the twentieth century with a choice, to harness the Industrial Revolution to our values of free enterprise, conservation, and human decency. Those choices made all the difference.

At the dawn of the twenty-first century a free people must now choose to shape the forces of the Information Age and the global society, to unleash the limitless potential of all our people, and, yes, to form a more perfect union.

When last we gathered, our march to this new future seemed less certain than it does today. We vowed then to set a clear course to renew our nation.

In these four years, we have been touched by tragedy, exhilarated by challenge, strengthened by achievement. America stands alone as the world's indispensable nation. Once again, our economy is the strongest on Earth. Once again, we are building stronger families, thriving communities, better educational opportunities, a cleaner environment. Problems that once seemed destined to deepen now bend to our efforts: our streets are safer and record numbers of our fellow citizens have moved from welfare to work.

And once again, we have resolved for our time a great debate over the role of government. Today we can declare: Government is not the problem, and government is not the solution. We, the American people, we are the solution. Our founders understood that well and gave us a democracy strong enough to endure for centuries, flexible enough to face our common challenges and advance our common dreams in each new day.

As times change, so government must change. We need a new government for a new century—humble enough not to try to solve all our problems for us, but strong enough to give us the tools to solve our problems for ourselves; a government that is smaller, lives within its means, and does more with less. Yet where it can stand up for our values and interests in the world, and where it can give Americans the power to make a real difference in their everyday lives, government should do more, not less. The preeminent mission of our new government is to give all Americans an opportunity, not a guarantee, but a real opportunity to build better lives.

Beyond that, my fellow citizens, the future is up to us. Our Founders taught us that the preservation of our liberty and our union depends upon responsible citizenship. And we need a new sense of responsibility for a new century. There is work to do, work that government alone cannot do: teaching children to read; hiring people off welfare rolls; coming out from behind locked doors and shuttered windows to help reclaim our streets from drugs and gangs and crime; taking time out of our own lives to serve others.

Each and every one of us, in our own way, must assume personal responsibility, not only for ourselves and our families, but for our neighbors and our nation. Our greatest responsibility is to embrace a new spirit of community for a new century. For any one of us to succeed, we must succeed as one America.

The challenge of our past remains the challenge of our future—will we be one nation, one people, with one common destiny, or not? Will we all come together, or come apart?

The divide of race has been America's constant curse. And each new wave of immigrants gives new targets to old prejudices. Prejudice and contempt, cloaked in the pretense of religious or political con-

President Clinton meets Senegalese villagers during a twelve-day visit to Africa in 1998—the first extended trip to the continent by a sitting U.S. head of state.

viction are no different. These forces have nearly destroyed our nation in the past. They plague us still. They fuel the fanaticism of terror. And they torment the lives of millions in fractured nations all around the world.

These obsessions cripple both those who hate and, of course, those who are hated, robbing both of what they might become. We cannot, we will not, succumb to the dark impulses that lurk in the far regions of the soul everywhere. We shall overcome them. And we shall replace them with the generous spirit of a people who feel at home with one another.

Our rich texture of racial, religious, and political diversity will be a Godsend in the twenty-first century. Great rewards will come to those who can live together, learn together, work together, forge new ties that bind together.

As this new era approaches we can already see its broad outlines. Ten years ago, the Internet was the mystical province of physicists; today, it is a commonplace encyclopedia for millions of schoolchildren. Scientists now are decoding the blueprint of human life. Cures for our most feared illnesses seem close at hand.

The world is no longer divided into two hostile camps. Instead, now we are building bonds with nations that once were our adversaries. Growing connections of commerce and culture give us a chance to lift the fortunes and spirits of people the world over. And for the very first time in all of history, more people on this planet live under democracy than dictatorship.

My fellow Americans, as we look back at this remarkable century, we may ask, can we hope not just to follow, but even to surpass the achievements of the twentieth century in America and to avoid the awful bloodshed that stained its legacy? To that question, every American here and every American in our land today must answer a resounding "Yes."

This is the heart of our task. With a new vision of government, a new sense of responsibility, a new spirit of community, we will sustain America's journey. The promise we sought in a new land we will find again in a land of new promise.

In this new land, education will be every citizen's most prized possession. Our schools will have the highest standards in the world, igniting the spark of possibility in the eyes of every girl and every boy. And the doors of higher education will be open to all. The knowledge and power of the Information Age will be within reach not just of the few, but of every classroom, every library, every child. Parents and children will have time not only to work, but to read and play together. And the plans they make at their kitchen table will be those of a better home, a better job, the certain chance to go to college.

Our streets will echo again with the laughter of

our children, because no one will try to shoot them or sell them drugs anymore. Everyone who can work, will work, with today's permanent under class part of tomorrow's growing middle class. New miracles of medicine at last will reach not only those who can claim care now, but the children and hardworking families too long denied.

We will stand mighty for peace and freedom, and maintain a strong defense against terror and destruction. Our children will sleep free from the threat of nuclear, chemical, or biological weapons. Ports and airports, farms and factories will thrive with trade and innovation and ideas. And the world's greatest democracy will lead a whole world of democracies.

Our land of new promise will be a nation that meets its obligations, a nation that balances its budget, but never loses the balance of its values. A nation where our grandparents have secure retirement and health care, and their grandchildren know we have made the reforms necessary to sustain those benefits for their time. A nation that fortifies the world's most productive economy even as it protects the great natural bounty of our water, air, and majestic land.

And in this land of new promise, we will have reformed our politics so that the voice of the people will always speak louder than the din of narrow interests, regaining the participation and deserving the trust of all Americans.

Fellow citizens, let us build that America, a nation ever moving forward toward realizing the full potential of all its citizens. Prosperity and power, yes, they are important, and we must maintain them. But let us never forget: The greatest progress we have made, and the greatest progress we have yet to make, is in the human heart. In the end, all the world's wealth and a thousand armies are no match for the strength and decency of the human spirit.

Thirty-four years ago, the man whose life we celebrate today[1] spoke to us down there, at the other end of this Mall, in words that moved the conscience of a nation. Like a prophet of old, he told of his dream that one day America would rise up and treat all its citizens as equals before the law and in the heart. Martin Luther King's dream was the American Dream. His quest is our quest: the ceaseless striving to live out our true creed. Our history has been built on such dreams and labors. And by our dreams and labors we will redeem the promise of America in the twenty-first century.

To that effort I pledge all my strength and every power of my office. I ask the members of Congress here to join in that pledge. The American people returned to office a president of one party and a

---

1. January 20, 1997, was Martin Luther King Jr. Day. Civil rights leader King (1929–68) gave his famous "I have a dream" speech on the Washington Mall, August 28, 1963.

America celebrates the new millennium with fireworks at the Washington Monument, Washington, D.C., January 1, 2000.

Congress of another. Surely, they did not do this to advance the politics of petty bickering and extreme partisanship they plainly deplore. No, they call on us instead to be repairers of the breach, and to move on with America's mission.

America demands and deserves big things from us, and nothing big ever came from being small. Let us remember the timeless wisdom of Cardinal Bernardin, when facing the end of his own life.[2] He said, "It is wrong to waste the precious gift of time, on acrimony and division."

Fellow citizens, we must not waste the precious gift of this time. For all of us are on that same journey of our lives, and our journey, too, will come to an end. But the journey of our America must go on.

And so, my fellow Americans, we must be strong, for there is much to dare. The demands of our time are great and they are different. Let us meet them with faith and courage, with patience and a grateful and happy heart. Let us shape the hope of this day into the noblest chapter in our history. Yes, let us build our bridge. A bridge wide enough and strong enough for every American to cross over to a blessed land of new promise.

May those generations whose faces we cannot yet see, whose names we may never know, say of us

---

2. Joseph Cardinal Bernardin (1928–96), Roman Catholic archbishop of Chicago, died of cancer November 14, 1996.

here that we led our beloved land into a new century with the American Dream alive for all her children; with the American promise of a more perfect union a reality for all her people; with America's bright flame of freedom spreading throughout all the world.

From the height of this place and the summit of this century, let us go forth. May God strengthen our hands for the good work ahead, and always, always bless our America.

George Walker Bush

43rd President of the United States

2001–

George Walker Bush

BORN: July 6, 1946, New Haven, Conn.
MARRIED: Laura Welch, Nov. 5, 1977; two children
PARTY: Republican
EDUCATION: Public grammar schools in Texas;
Phillips Academy; Yale University (1968); Harvard
Business School (1975).

CAREER:
Texas Air National Guard; oil business; political campaign worker; unsuccessful run for Congress (1978);
managing partner of the Texas Rangers baseball team;
Texas governor (1995–2000); president (2001–).

PRESIDENTIAL CAMPAIGNS:
2000: Bested Senator John McCain of Arizona and
Steve Forbes, publisher and financier, in bitter primar-
ies. With Dick Cheney, another western oilman, to
oppose Democratic ticket of Vice President Al Gore
and Connecticut Senator Joseph Lieberman, the first
Jewish candidate.
2004: Democratic senators John Kerry of Massachusetts
and John Edwards of South Carolina tried to unseat
Bush/Cheney. Vietnam was as much an issue as Iraq,
with decorated veteran Kerry coming under attack for
fiercely opposing the war on his return home. Bush
won by 3,500,000 votes.

President George W. and Laura Bush dance at an inaugural ball,
January 20, 2005.

Introduction

George W. Bush was the first son of a former president to reach the White House since John Quincy Adams in 1825. Although born and educated in New England, Bush grew up in Midland, Texas, and considered himself a westerner. People liked his warmth and grace and also his humor, which often included high jinks. Early, he showed a yen for politics, working in numerous campaigns—all of them ending in defeat. Not successful in the oil business, he soon was helping his father get elected president in 1988.

Now Bush turned to his great love, baseball. Skilled at acquiring investors, he built a partnership that bought the Texas Rangers. Still, politics remained a deep interest and, in 1993, he was elected Texas governor.

By 2000, he had his eyes on the presidency. The outcome of that election was the most controversial since 1876. Gore had 500,000 more votes than Bush but was one vote short of a majority in the Electoral College. The outcome depended on recounting the votes in Florida. The Supreme Court by a five-to-four partisan vote upheld the certification of the Florida returns, giving the election to Bush.

In his inaugural, Bush said a friendly word about Gore's grace. He also recognized that the divisions in the Nation were not only political but also economic and social.

George Walker Bush
First Inaugural Address

Saturday, January 20, 2001

President Clinton, distinguished guests and my fellow citizens:

The peaceful transfer of authority is rare in history, yet common in our country. With a simple oath, we affirm old traditions and make new beginnings.

As I begin, I thank President Clinton for his service to our nation; and I thank Vice President Gore[1] for a contest conducted with spirit and ended with grace.

I am honored and humbled to stand here, where so many of America's leaders have come before me, and so many will follow.

We have a place, all of us, in a long story. A story we continue, but whose end we will not see. It is the story of a new world that became a friend and liberator of the old, a story of a slave-holding society that became a servant of freedom, the story of a power that went into the world to protect but not possess, to defend but not to conquer. It is the American story. A story of flawed and fallible people, united across the generations by grand and enduring ideals. The grandest of these ideals is an unfolding Ameri-

---

1. Albert Arnold Gore Jr. (1948–   ), forty-fifth vice president, 1993–2001.

can promise that everyone belongs, that everyone deserves a chance, that no insignificant person was ever born. Americans are called upon to enact this promise in our lives and in our laws; and though our Nation has sometimes halted, and sometimes delayed, we must follow no other course.

Through much of the last century, America's faith in freedom and democracy was a rock in a raging sea. Now it is a seed upon the wind, taking root in many nations. Our democratic faith is more than the creed of our country, it is the inborn hope of our humanity, an ideal we carry but do not own, a trust we bear and pass along; and even after nearly 225 years, we have a long way yet to travel.

While many of our citizens prosper, others doubt the promise, even the justice, of our own country. The ambitions of some Americans are limited by failing schools and hidden prejudice and the circumstances of their birth; and sometimes our differences run so deep, it seems we share a continent, but not a country. We do not accept this, and we will not allow it. Our unity, our union, is the serious work of leaders and citizens in every generation; and this is my solemn pledge, "I will work to build a single nation of justice and opportunity." I know this is in our reach because we are guided by a power larger than ourselves who creates us equal in His image and we are confident in principles that unite and lead us onward.

America has never been united by blood or birth or soil. We are bound by ideals that move us beyond our backgrounds, lift us above our interests and teach us what it means to be citizens. Every child must be taught these principles. Every citizen must uphold them; and every immigrant, by embracing these ideals, makes our country more, not less, American.

Today, we affirm a new commitment to live out our Nation's promise through civility, courage, compassion, and character. America, at its best, matches a commitment to principle with a concern for civility. A civil society demands from each of us good will and respect, fair dealing and forgiveness. Some seem to believe that our politics can afford to be petty because, in a time of peace, the stakes of our debates appear small. But the stakes for America are never small. If our country does not lead the cause of freedom, it will not be led. If we do not turn the hearts of children toward knowledge and character, we will lose their gifts and undermine their idealism. If we permit our economy to drift and decline, the vulnerable will suffer most. We must live up to the calling we share. Civility is not a tactic or a sentiment. It is the determined choice of trust over cynicism, of community over chaos. This commitment, if we keep it, is a way to shared accomplishment.

America, at its best, is also courageous. Our national courage has been clear in times of depression and war, when defending common dangers defined our common good. Now we must choose if the example of our fathers and mothers will inspire us or condemn us. We must show courage in a time of blessing by confronting problems instead of passing them on to future generations.

Together, we will reclaim America's schools, before ignorance and apathy claim more young lives; we will reform Social Security and Medicare, sparing our children from struggles we have the power to prevent; we will reduce taxes, to recover the momentum of our economy and reward the effort and enterprise of working Americans; we will build our defenses beyond challenge, lest weakness invite challenge; and we will confront weapons of mass destruction, so that a new century is spared new horrors.

The enemies of liberty and our country should make no mistake, America remains engaged in the world by history and by choice, shaping a balance of power that favors freedom. We will defend our allies and our interests; we will show purpose without arrogance; we will meet aggression and bad faith with resolve and strength; and to all nations, we will speak for the values that gave our Nation birth.

America, at its best, is compassionate. In the quiet of American conscience, we know that deep, persistent poverty is unworthy of our Nation's promise. Whatever our views of its cause, we can

The second plane crashes into the south tower of the World Trade Center while the north tower burns from the first terrorist attack, New York City, September 11, 2001.

367

agree that children at risk are not at fault. Abandonment and abuse are not acts of God, they are failures of love. The proliferation of prisons, however
necessary, is no substitute for hope and order in our
souls. Where there is suffering, there is duty. Americans in need are not strangers, they are citizens, not
problems, but priorities, and all of us are diminished when any are hopeless. Government has great
responsibilities for public safety and public health,
for civil rights and common schools. Yet compassion is the work of a nation, not just a government.
Some needs and hurts are so deep they will only
respond to a mentor's touch or a pastor's prayer.
Church and charity, synagogue and mosque lend
our communities their humanity, and they will
have an honored place in our plans and in our laws.
Many in our country do not know the pain of
poverty, but we can listen to those who do. I can
pledge our nation to a goal: When we see that
wounded traveler on the road to Jericho, we will
not pass to the other side.[2]

America, at its best, is a place where personal
responsibility is valued and expected. Encouraging
responsibility is not a search for scapegoats, it is a
call to conscience. Though it requires sacrifice, it
brings a deeper fulfillment. We find the fullness of
life not only in options, but in commitments. We

---

2. Reference to the parable of the Good Samaritan, Luke 10:25–37.

President George W. Bush, atop the rubble at Ground Zero in New York City, rallies rescue workers, September 14, 2001.

find that children and community are the commitments that set us free. Our public interest depends on private character, on civic duty and family bonds and basic fairness, on uncounted, unhonored acts of decency which give direction to our freedom. Sometimes in life we are called to do great things. But as a saint of our times[3] has said, every day we are called to do small things with great love. The most important tasks of a democracy are done by everyone. I will live and lead by these principles, "to advance my convictions with civility, to pursue the public interest with courage, to speak for greater justice and compassion, to call for responsibility and try to live it as well." In all of these ways, I will bring the values of our history to the care of our times.

What you do is as important as anything government does. I ask you to seek a common good beyond your comfort; to defend needed reforms against easy attacks; to serve your Nation, beginning with your neighbor. I ask you to be citizens. Citizens, not spectators; citizens, not subjects; responsible citizens, building communities of service and a nation of character.

Americans are generous and strong and decent, not because we believe in ourselves, but because we

---

3. Mother Teresa's Nobel Lecture, December 11, 1979. Mother Teresa (née Agnes Gonxha Bojaxhiu, 1910–97) founded the Missionaries of Charity in India. She was beatified in 2003.

hold beliefs beyond ourselves. When this spirit of citizenship is missing, no government program can replace it. When this spirit is present, no wrong can stand against it.

After the Declaration of Independence was signed, Virginia statesman John Page[4] wrote to Thomas Jefferson, "We know the race is not to the swift nor the battle to the strong. Do you not think an angel rides in the whirlwind and directs this storm?" Much time has passed since Jefferson arrived for his inauguration. The years and changes accumulate, but the themes of this day he would know, "our nation's grand story of courage and its simple dream of dignity."

We are not this story's author, who fills time and eternity with His purpose. Yet His purpose is achieved in our duty, and our duty is fulfilled in service to one another. Never tiring, never yielding, never finishing, we renew that purpose today; to make our country more just and generous; to affirm the dignity of our lives and every life.

This work continues. This story goes on. And an angel still rides in the whirlwind and directs this storm.

God bless you all, and God bless America.

---

4. John Page (1744–1808) helped frame Virginia's constitution, represented the state in Congress, and eventually became governor.

A U.S. Marine stands guard in the center of Baghdad, Iraq, April 11, 2003.

INTRODUCTION

The terrorist attack on America on September 11, 2001, was a defining moment for America and for President Bush. It changed his focus and priorities. But the country's high respect for him after 9/11 had diminished by 2004. The loss of confidence was largely due to anxiety over the war in Iraq and to the failure to find "weapons of mass destruction"—the administration's reason for invading Iraq.

Bush campaigned vigorously and defended his policies. His opponent, Senator John Kerry, denounced Bush for unreliable intelligence reports and promised to rebuild international alliances that had been weakened by hostility to the war. Domestically, Bush defended his tax program and appealed strongly to conservatives on cultural issues. The electoral vote this time hinged on Ohio, which finally registered for Bush.

President Bush's oath of office was administered by a gravely ill Chief Justice William Rehnquist, who remained on the scene for only ten minutes. The president in his inaugural, apparently aiming for national unity, made no mention of Iraq and little of the issues that he had dwelt upon in the campaign. Instead, he provided an idealist's view—reminiscent of Woodrow Wilson's—of America's brand of freedom being a desirable goal for all peoples. The president's delivery, however, lacked the forcefulness that Kennedy and Franklin Roosevelt had shown in memorable inaugurals.

George Walker Bush
Second Inaugural Address

Thursday, January 20, 2005

Vice President Cheney, Mr. Chief Justice, President Carter, President Bush, President Clinton,[1] members of the United States Congress, reverend clergy, distinguished guests, fellow citizens:

On this day, prescribed by law and marked by ceremony, we celebrate the durable wisdom of our Constitution and recall the deep commitments that unite our country. I am grateful for the honor of this hour, mindful of the consequential times in which we live, and determined to fulfill the oath that I have sworn and you have witnessed.

At this second gathering, our duties are defined not by the words I use but by the history we have seen together. For a half a century, America defended our own freedom by standing watch on distant borders. After the shipwreck of communism came years of relative quiet, years of repose, years of sabbatical, and then there came a day of fire.[2]

We have seen our vulnerability, and we have seen

---

1. Richard Bruce Cheney (1941–), forty-sixth vice president; William Hubbs Rehnquist (1924–2005), chief justice of the United States, 1986– ; President James Earl Carter Jr.; President George Herbert Walker Bush; President William Jefferson Clinton.
2. September 11, 2001: Terrorists flew planes into the World Trade Center, New York, New York, and the Pentagon, Arlington, Vir-

its deepest source. For as long as whole regions of the world simmer in resentment and tyranny, prone to ideologies that feed hatred and excuse murder, violence will gather and multiply in destructive power and cross the most defended borders and raise a mortal threat. There is only one force of history that can break the reign of hatred and resentment and expose the pretensions of tyrants and reward the hopes of the decent and tolerant, and that is the force of human freedom.

We are led, by events and common sense, to one conclusion: The survival of liberty in our land increasingly depends on the success of liberty in other lands. The best hope for peace in our world is the expansion of freedom in all the world.

America's vital interests and our deepest beliefs are now one. From the day of our founding, we have proclaimed that every man and woman on this earth has rights and dignity and matchless value, because they bear the image of the Maker of heaven and Earth. Across the generations, we have proclaimed the imperative of self-government, because no one is fit to be a master and no one deserves to be a slave.[3] Advancing these ideals is the mission that created

ginia, and were forced to crash a plane into the ground near Shanksville, Pennsylvania.
3. Paraphrase of a statement by Abraham Lincoln (1809–65), sixteenth president of the United States: "As I would not be a slave, so I would not be a master," letter fragment, c. August 1, 1858.

our Nation. It is the honorable achievement of our fathers. Now, it is the urgent requirement of our Nation's security and the calling of our time.

So it is the policy of the United States to seek and support the growth of democratic movements and institutions in every nation and culture, with the ultimate goal of ending tyranny in our world. This is not primarily the task of arms, though we will defend ourselves and our friends by force of arms when necessary. Freedom, by its nature, must be chosen and defended by citizens and sustained by the rule of law and the protection of minorities. And when the soul of a nation finally speaks, the institutions that arise may reflect customs and traditions very different from our own. America will not impose our own style of government on the unwilling. Our goal instead is to help others find their own voice, attain their own freedom, and make their own way.

The great objective of ending tyranny is the concentrated work of generations. The difficulty of the task is no excuse for avoiding it. America's influence is not unlimited, but fortunately for the oppressed, America's influence is considerable and we will use it confidently in freedom's cause.

My most solemn duty is to protect this Nation and its people from further attacks and emerging threats. Some have unwisely chosen to test America's resolve, and have found it firm. We will persistently clarify the choice before every ruler and every nation, the moral choice between oppression, which is always wrong, and freedom, which is eternally right.

America will not pretend that jailed dissidents prefer their chains or that women welcome humiliation and servitude or that any human being aspires to live at the mercy of bullies. We will encourage reform in other governments by making clear that success in our relations will require the decent treatment of their own people. America's belief in human dignity will guide our policies. Yet rights must be more than the grudging concessions of dictators. They are secured by free dissent and the participation of the governed. In the long run, there is no justice without freedom, and there can be no human rights without human liberty.

Some, I know, have questioned the global appeal of liberty, though this time in history, four decades defined by the swiftest advance of freedom ever seen, is an odd time for doubt. Americans, of all people, should never be surprised by the power of our ideals. Eventually, the call of freedom comes to every mind and every soul. We do not accept the existence of permanent tyranny because we do not accept the possibility of permanent slavery. Liberty will come to those who love it.

Today, America speaks anew to the peoples of the world. All who live in tyranny and hopelessness can know: The United States will not ignore your oppression or excuse your oppressors. When you stand for your liberty, we will stand with you.

Democratic reformers facing repression, prison, or exile can know: America sees you for who you are, the future leaders of your free country.

The rulers of outlaw regimes can know that we still believe as Abraham Lincoln did: "Those who deny freedom to others deserve it not for themselves and, under the rule of a just God, cannot long retain it."[4]

The leaders of governments with long habits of control need to know: To serve your people, you must learn to trust them. Start on this journey of progress and justice, and America will walk at your side.

And all the allies of the United States can know: We honor your friendship; we rely on your counsel; and we depend on your help. Division among free nations is a primary goal of freedom's enemies. The concerted effort of free nations to promote democracy is a prelude to our enemies' defeat.

Today I also speak anew to my fellow citizens. From all of you I have asked patience in the hard task of securing America, which you have granted in good measure. Our country has accepted obligations that are difficult to fulfill and would be dis-

---

4. Abraham Lincoln, letter to Henry L. Pierce and others, April 6, 1859.

New Orleans residents waded through Canal Street after Hurricane Katrina slammed the Gulf Coast, August 30, 2005.

honorable to abandon. Yet, because we have acted in the great liberating tradition of this Nation, tens of millions have achieved their freedom. And as hope kindles hope, millions more will find it. By our efforts, we have lit a fire as well, a fire in the minds of men. It warms those who feel its power. It burns those who fight its progress. And one day this untamed fire of freedom will reach the darkest corners of our world.

A few Americans have accepted the hardest duties in this cause, in the quiet work of intelligence and diplomacy, the idealistic work of helping raise up free governments, the dangerous and necessary work of fighting our enemies. Some have shown their devotion to our country in deaths that honored their whole lives, and we will always honor their names and their sacrifice.

All Americans have witnessed this idealism and some for the first time. I ask our youngest citizens to believe the evidence of your eyes. You have seen duty and allegiance in the determined faces of our soldiers. You have seen that life is fragile and evil is real and courage triumphs. Make the choice to serve in a cause larger than your wants, larger than yourself, and in your days you will add not just to the wealth of our country but to its character.

America has need of idealism and courage because we have essential work at home, the unfinished work of American freedom. In a world moving toward liberty, we are determined to show the meaning and promise of liberty.

In America's ideal of freedom, citizens find the dignity and security of economic independence instead of laboring on the edge of subsistence. This is the broader definition of liberty that motivated the Homestead Act,[5] the Social Security Act,[6] and the GI Bill of Rights.[7] And now we will extend this vision by reforming great institutions to serve the needs of our time. To give every American a stake in the promise and future of our country, we will bring the highest standards to our schools and build an ownership society. We will widen the ownership of homes and businesses, retirement savings, and health insurance, preparing our people for the challenges of life in a free society. By making every citizen an agent of his or her own destiny, we will give our fellow Americans greater freedom from want and fear and make our society more prosperous and just and equal.

---

5. The Homestead Act of 1862, signed by Abraham Lincoln, opened 270 million acres of public land to settlement. A head of household, 21 years or older, could claim a 160-acre parcel by living on it, building a home, making improvements, and farming it for five years.
6. The Social Security Act of 1935, signed by Franklin Roosevelt, provided for a system of old-age insurance for workers and survivor benefits for widows and children of insured workers.
7. The GI Bill of Rights of 1944, signed by Franklin Roosevelt, provided veterans with unemployment benefits, education assistance, and low-interest loans for homes, farms, and small businesses.

In America's ideal of freedom, the public interest depends on private character, on integrity and tolerance toward others and the rule of conscience in our own lives. Self-government relies, in the end, on the governing of the self. That edifice of character is built in families, supported by communities with standards, and sustained in our national life by the truths of Sinai, the Sermon on the Mount, the words of the Koran, and the varied faiths of our people. Americans move forward in every generation by reaffirming all that is good and true that came before, ideals of justice and conduct that are the same yesterday, today, and forever.

In America's ideal of freedom, the exercise of rights is ennobled by service and mercy and a heart for the weak. Liberty for all does not mean independence from one another. Our Nation relies on men and women who look after a neighbor and surround the lost with love. Americans, at our best, value the life we see in one another and must always remember that even the unwanted have worth. And our country must abandon all the habits of racism, because we cannot carry the message of freedom and the baggage of bigotry at the same time.

From the perspective of a single day, including this day of dedication, the issues and questions before our country are many. From the viewpoint of centuries, the questions that come to us are narrowed and few. Did our generation advance the cause of freedom? And did our character bring credit to that cause?

These questions that judge us also unite us, because Americans of every party and background, Americans by choice and by birth are bound to one another in the cause of freedom. We have known divisions, which must be healed to move forward in great purposes, and I will strive in good faith to heal them. Yet those divisions do not define America. We felt the unity and fellowship of our Nation when freedom came under attack, and our response came like a single hand over a single heart. And we can feel that same unity and pride whenever America acts for good and the victims of disaster are given hope and the unjust encounter justice and the captives are set free.

We go forward with complete confidence in the eventual triumph of freedom, not because history runs on the wheels of inevitability—it is human choices that move events; not because we consider ourselves a chosen nation—God moves and chooses as He wills. We have confidence because freedom is the permanent hope of mankind, the hunger in dark places, the longing of the soul. When our Founders declared a new order of the ages, when soldiers died in wave upon wave for a union based on liberty, when citizens marched in peaceful outrage under the banner "Freedom Now," they were acting on an ancient hope that is meant to be fulfilled. History has an ebb and flow of justice, but history also has a visible direction, set by liberty and the Author of Liberty.

When the Declaration of Independence was first read in public and the Liberty Bell was sounded in celebration, a witness said, "It rang as if it meant something." In our time, it means something still. America, in this young century, proclaims liberty throughout all the world and to all the inhabitants thereof. Renewed in our strength, tested but not weary, we are ready for the greatest achievements in the history of freedom.

May God bless you, and may He watch over the United States of America.

List of The Lakeside Classics

The Lakeside Classics

The Lakeside Classics

The Lakeside Classics

The Lakeside Classics

The Presidential Seal

The first president to use the presidential seal was Ruther-ford B. Hayes, who displayed on White House invitations in 1880. The design had the head of an eagle turned to the viewer's right, toward the talon holding the arrows of war.

In 1944, President Franklin D. Roosevelt decided to update the design. The naval aide sketching the redesign noted the incorrect position of the eagle's head, which in heraldic eagles faces left. President Harry S. Truman made the change on October 26, 1945.

The presidential seal was updated in 1960, following the admission of Alaska and Hawaii as the forty-ninth and fiftieth states.

IMAGE CREDITS

March of Dimes: *211*

National Aeronautics and Space Administration: *258*

National Archives and Records Administration: *49*; *109*; *161*, Clem Albers, photographer; *163*; *169*; *179*, Lt. Victor Jorgensen, photographer; *239*; *247*; *265*

National Baseball Hall of Fame Library, Cooperstown, New York: *103*

Naval Historical Foundation: *158*

The Panama Gateway by Joseph Bucklin Bishop, [New York: Charles Scribner's Sons, 1913]: *23*

Ronald Reagan Presidential Library: *289*, *292*, *300*

St. Louis Globe-Democrat Archives of the St. Louis Mercantile Library, University of Missouri-St. Louis: *94*, *173*

Seattle-King County Department of Public Health Photograph Files (112-275), King County Archives: *114*

Smithsonian Institution Photo No. 93-10316-28: *337*

U.S. Air Force: *176*

U.S. Marine Corps: *372*, Sgt. Joseph R. Chenelly, photographer

The White House: *219*; *361*, Susan Sterner, photographer; *369*, Eric Draper, photographer

William J. Clinton Presidential Library: *351*

DESIGNED, TYPESET, PRINTED, BOUND, AND DISTRIBUTED BY
R.R. DONNELLEY & SONS COMPANY

COMPOSITION:
ALLENTOWN DIGITAL SERVICES,
ALLENTOWN, PENNSYLVANIA

SCANNING AND IMAGE PROOFING:
ELGIN PREMEDIA CENTER,
ELGIN, ILLINOIS

COMPUTER TO PLATES, PRINTING, AND BINDING:
RR DONNELLEY PRINT PLANT, CRAWFORDSVILLE, INDIANA

ADDRESSING AND MAILING:
MOORE WALLACE RESPONSE MARKETING SERVICES

WORLDWIDE DISTRIBUTION:
RR DONNELLEY LOGISTICS

BODY TYPEFACE:
11/12.85 POINT GARAMOND

PAPER STOCK:
50-POUND WHITE LAKESIDE CLASSICS,
BY GLATFELTER

CLOTH:
ARRESTOX VELLUM, LAKESIDE GREEN,
BY HOLLISTON MILLS, INC.

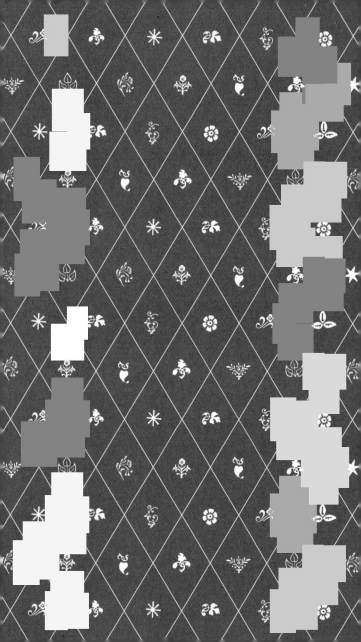